The Nature of Belonging

Groundings in the Earth of Daily Life

Vonnie Roudette

iUniverse, Inc.
Bloomington

The Nature of Belonging

Copyright © 2011 by Vonnie Roudette

All rights reserved. No part of this book may be used or reproduced by any means, graphic, electronic, or mechanical, including photocopying, recording, taping or by any information storage retrieval system without the written permission of the publisher except in the case of brief quotations embodied in critical articles and reviews.

The views expressed in this work are solely those of the author and do not necessarily reflect the views of the publisher, and the publisher hereby disclaims any responsibility for them.

iUniverse books may be ordered through booksellers or by contacting:

iUniverse
1663 Liberty Drive
Bloomington, IN 47403
www.iuniverse.com
1-800-Authors (1-800-288-4677)

Because of the dynamic nature of the Internet, any web addresses or links contained in this book may have changed since publication and may no longer be valid.

Any people depicted in stock imagery provided by Thinkstock are models, and such images are being used for illustrative purposes only.

Certain stock imagery © Thinkstock.

ISBN: 978-1-4620-0658-8 (sc)
ISBN: 978-1-4620-0659-5 (hc)
ISBN: 978-1-4620-0660-1 (ebk)

Library of Congress Control Number: 2011905262

Printed in the United States of America

iUniverse rev. date: 01/04/2012

To Aiko and Marlon, the islands' youth and
All whose Hearts hold dear the Nature of our Valley.

Contents

FOREWORD - by Oscar Allen xii

OPEN SHORES - Preamble xvi

1. RESOLUTE MOON - January 1
   Creativity in Daily life 4
   The Cost of Naturalness 8
   The Seeds of Culture 11
   Purposeful Resolutions 14
   Message from the Resolute Moon 19

2. ANCESTRAL MOON - Februa 21
   The Impulse of Black History 25
   Inheriting Wisdom of the Youth 29
   In the Hundreds 32
   Plot to Freedom 36
   Message from the Ancestral Moon 39

3. BIRTHING MOON - March 41
   National Hero or Dangerous Revolutionary? 45
   Digging to Bury Heroes 48
   The Most Precious Possession 51
   A Woman's Years – Celebrating International
      Women's Day 2009 55
   Message from the Birthing Moon 63

4. EARTH MOON - April 65
   The Greatest of Wastes 68
   Human Beings – an Endangered Species? 71
   Coastal Desert 75

  Earth Day Remembrance 78
  Message from the Earth Moon 83

5. SEA WATER MOON - May 85
  Childhood Memories are made of this. 88
  Hungry for Poverty 92
  Tracks and Pathways 96
  Mothers' Day of Healing 99
  Message from the Sea Water Moon 103

6. MANGO MOON - June 105
  Healthy Common Sense: Virtuous Gardening 108
  Graduates of Life 111
  Wellness Grown at Home 114
  The Stately Kitchen Garden 118
  Message from the Mango Moon 121

7. CREATIVE MOON - July 123
  The Art of Carnival 126
  You Can Eat Culture!. 132
  A Mindless Feast? 136
  An Empty Cultural Package 139
  Message from the Creative Moon 143

8. MOUNTAIN SPRING MOON - August 145
  None But Ourselves 148
  Champions of Integration 151
  Message from the Mountain 156
  Filed Away Where? 159
  Message from the Mountain Spring Moon 165

9. BOUNTIFUL MOON - September 167
  A Modest Culture 171
  Food: Activism or Praxis? 175
  Farmer in the Diaspora 179
  A National Living Treasure 182
  Message from the Bountiful Moon 187

10. FREE SPIRIT MOON - October 189
    The Homecoming 192
    In Dependence 197
    Social Cohesion or Generational Suffering? 202
    Sister Pat, Moving Spirit 206
    Message from the Free Spirit Moon 209

11. FOREST RIVER MOON - November 211
    Homeless Island 215
    A Nation of Designers 219
    Fresh Growth: A natural development 224
    Soil Searching 228
    Message from the Forest River Moon 231

12. RETURNING MOON - December 233
    Our Caribbean Sister 236
    I. Culture as Experience 236
    II. Wellness Below the Surface 239
    A Crime to be Happy 242
    Happy Cash Returns! 245
    Message from the Returning Moon 251

13. BLUE MOON 253
    Timeless Moon 256
    Test of Natural Intelligence 260
    The Culture Haven 264
    Natural Steps to Belonging: Practical Action
      Sequences for Self-Discovery and Community
      Healing. 268
    Message from the Blue Moon 273

14. AFTERWORD: A Life of Nature Ramblings 275

Acknowledgements

I have mountains to thank, not least of all the mountains of St. Vincent and Dominica that have nurtured me through many days of reflective solitude. I give immense thanks to all young people on whose creative path I have been privileged to be invited and who have been, as part of nature, my greatest teachers; they inspire hope; they are the precious resource of our community and are our treasures. Like my own children, they are my friends and family as I follow events in their lives with deep affection and connection.

Instrumental in the becoming of this book was Eloise Gonsalves who escorted me to WE FM radio station in June 2004 and encouraged me through a nervous recording of what was to become, unbeknownst to us both, the first of many from which these essays were adapted. And my dear friends Rhonda King and Dr. Jules Ferdinand whose joint insistence to compile the manuscript outweighed my resistance to withdraw from other activities to undertake the task. My heartfelt respect for them both was the decisive factor in beginning the work and their unwavering support ensured its completion. I am also deeply grateful to Brother Oscar Allen whose gracious presence in the foreword flows through these pages, and to George Lamming, a beacon through the labyrinth of our multi-island culture.

I give boundless thanks to my father Clayton, who holds a continuously evolving belief in what is possible, and to my mother June, who overcame hurdles to tend my early imaginings. Peggy Carr, 'booops', Gary Peters and Ade, elevated creative empathies with whom, through shared pain and joy, I am inextricably bound. And my valley sister Brenda, who sheltered me through untold challenges with love and laughter. You are all gifts graciously bestowed. Our endless days of silent communication with nature hold boundless possibilities for a healing community embrace of our Caribbean integrity of practical wisdom and egoless connection with the landscape.

Foreword
by Oscar Allen

This anthology by an artist and designer is a work of passion. I would even venture to classify it as "evangelical", in the peculiar way that George Lamming describes CLR James, and himself as evangelists. The writer, Ms. Vonnie Roudette, has brought from her experiences on every continent, a finely crafted sense of belonging to the cosmos and to earth. While she writes of her hurting as she sees that the "widespread destruction of green life is ... damaging the planet's immune system ... (creating) a potentially fatal disorder of climate change", this collection of fifty-two essays is devoted to healing and wholeness without glossing over the lethal terror that mother earth is suffering. At one point Roudette refers to the poet John O'Donohue's discernment that:

> "The light that suffering leaves when it goes is a very precious light".

One feature of this book which fascinates me is its tangible 'Vincentianness'. Vonnie Roudette opens our eyes to see a truckload of prisoners in a new way. She chronicles the loss of Buccament beach through the shock of a beach-loving youth. She unveils the meaning of the mountain rainforest "just a few miles away from the sea". She uplifts the nearly invisible farmer who knows that "nature is a marvellous and awesome force by whose kind permission we survive on her bounty of water, earth and air". She touches on the potential and promise of our young people and she reminds us of Sister Pat Douglas, and Shake Keane. Behind all this, there is a dialogue in these pages between two or more ways of thinking. That is the point of the book; to share in real stories the Roudette compassion for life, for nature, for people who can become open to others. These essays are the personal testimony of an urgent, loving spirit.

It could be a fruitful way to read this book by taking the essays as Shake Keane prescribed: "One a week with water" paying attention to the Resolve in each piece.

Back in 1992, when Vonnie Roudette (and her son and daughter) arrived in St.Vincent and the Grenadines, her wandering spirit encountered the magnetic natural beauty of Youroumein and she has become rooted. Our soil has sustained her soul, and her soul reverences the soil. It is from that bounding of soil and soul that this book is born and Ms. Roudette confirms that she belongs with us, and our predicament is also hers. This spirited work, then, adds to the growing Vincentian output of literature, a novel volume that combines artistry, advocacy and testimony, and a different mode of belonging. Vonnie Roudette's book should trouble the waters and enrich the reader.

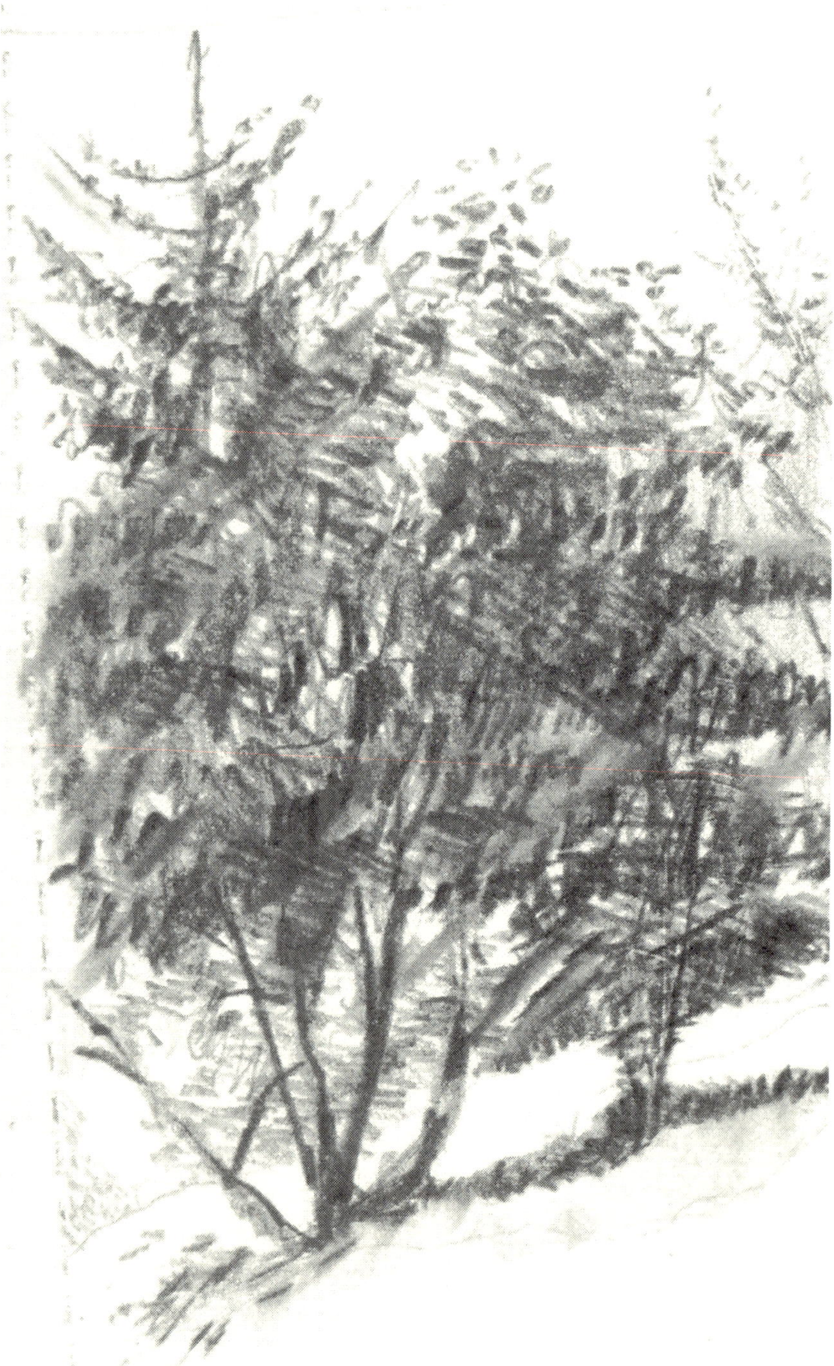

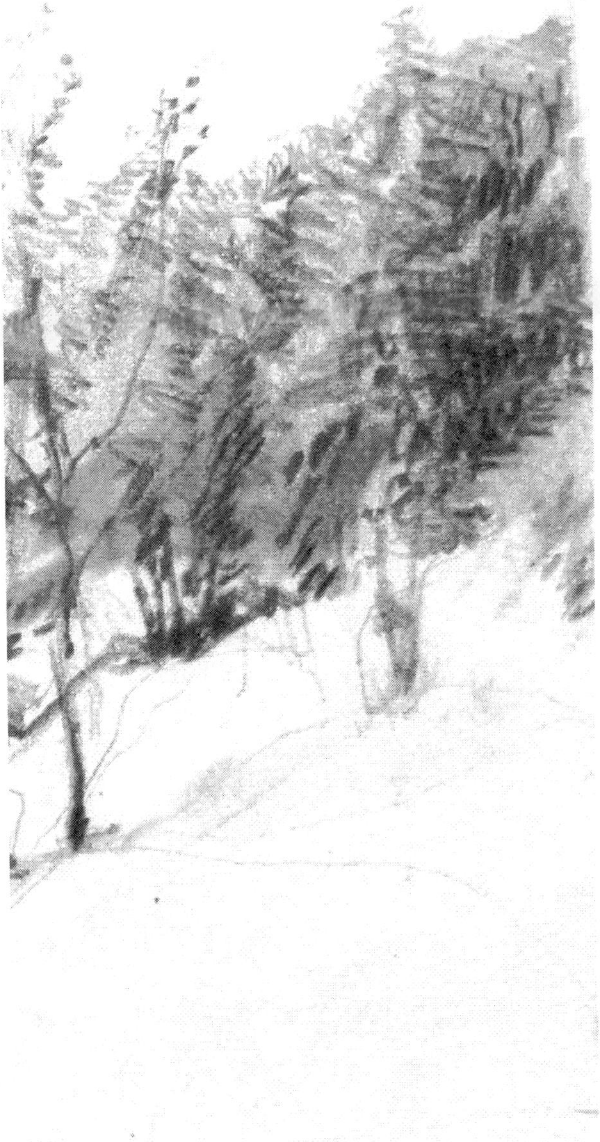

Open Shores

Preamble

This collection of short essays is compiled largely from five-minute weekly radio commentaries that were aired in St Vincent and the Grenadines on WEFM's 'Viewpoint' programme between June 2004 and June 2009.

With continual preparation and recording of these commentaries, I began to perceive the passing years as cyclical revolutions punctuated by repeating festivals and holidays. Sometimes, I would review what I wrote in previous years. In June 2009, I re-read my commentaries about Vincy Carnival and noticed that the comments made five years previously were still relevant.

As tempted as I was to repeat these commentaries out of convenience and necessity, I chose instead to express the reality of commentating once per week, year in year out, with a predictable regularity that in the spirit of creative non-conformity, I often sought to escape.

Listeners who tuned in over the years, encouraged me in times of doubt, and some seemed to value my humble offerings to a nation whose beauty and power is yet to be understood by its own; an island nation whose authentic fragments of intangible culture have not yet proven sufficient to weave a durable mantle to hand to its youth; an island where the people who belong to it, who were formed by and fed from the land and the mountains, by the rhythm of the sea and flow of rivers, have severed themselves from their roots of dignity and become attached instead to a flimsy and fickle culture that often leads them into despair with themselves and their sisters and brothers.

An island people whose ability to appreciate what is simple and profound strains to breaking point under the seduction of a culture that advertises superfluous things, suckling our children on the vastly flowing veins of corporate America filled with corpuscles of profit, drugs and alcohol. An island whose Liverty is indiscernible in the fog of self-seeking generated by most personal and political decisions.

As this island's inhabitants lead a life of escape from itself, a few turn towards her and pray that she, in her invisible glory, will stay strong for them, will continue to nurture and support the life and soul seam, just long enough for us to realize what it is we have before us but refuse to see.

As we scuffle in ignorance of our own island that sustains us, swollen by violence, by drugs of power, by arrogance and materialism, by criticism and downpression, sometimes a comment from a stranger has given me inspiration, energy and reaffirmation. This single comment can sustain me for a long time, so desperately do I cling to my belief that we are capable of another way of living, that there are others who long to see humanity in the eyes of our reflection. And who long to see that reflection in the eyes of their fellow islanders.

"Some may say I'm a dreamer but I am not the only one. "

My oft-held feelings are echoed in John Lennon's words engraved in the ground next to his seated statue in a Havana park. Like our Cuban family, my sisters and brothers of these little islands, let our dreams of island realization embrace the unifying power of sports and the arts that have taken our essence overseas; that have made our mark on others; that others have done more with than we have; that we have yet to discover in our children; that can give us strength and belief in ourselves.

After five years of producing weekly commentaries, I asked my listening audience to bear with me as I felt I had said more than enough over the years. I stepped aside to assess and analyse the path forward with respect to writing weekly viewpoint commentaries and to compile the material for this publication. This is a humble offering to the natural beauty of our homescape, in shared recognition of the desperate calling from Her for us to revive our tenacious spirits through healing Her soil, which is our life-blood hibernating beneath layers of harsh endurance.

In this vein, my life's work is to assist the passing of our creative environmental legacy onto the youth through the arts, on the land, in my heart. For they are simply the heart beat of our island, innocent victims of the rage that wells up within our bellies. Because of this rage that we inflict on each other, our children are born disadvantaged and yet in their innocence, are still connected to our islands, to the indigenous people who toiled for our liberation. Our children are born of the resilience and expression of our ancestors, and their spirits long as we all do, to reconnect with the umbilical beat of rainforest-fresh water, not drugs and alcohol within our veins: not hate and envy, but love and compassion: not greed and power, but gifts for our communities; not for individual desire but for the greater good.

The words on the following pages are a fraction of what evaporated in those weekly airings condensed on the page, inert unless transformed into action. Only you, the reader, can tell if I have succeeded in translating aspects of an intangible culture of feeling and experiences within the psyche of a passionate people, into words on the page. I felt the task impossible at times, bereft as I was of recourse to the vocal intonation and emphasis of the spoken word. I hope that the references to daily experiences that we share will ignite sufficient connection between us to lift words off the page into your thoughts that breathe our cultural connection. The ideas of precious islanders are many and marvellous, and will find form if we can listen to eachother with genuine appreciation, enabling us to proceed towards collective action for healing our communities.

The essays are presented in 'moon sections', in accordance with the flow of nature that generated them; each new moon offers an interlude of reflection- a drawing formed through active contemplation- that reveals insights into the nature of our belonging. The essays can be read at random, in succession, at weekly intervals or corresponding to moon phases that occur with regularity in the great natural order of the universe. A new beginning is often accompanied by resolutions, a Resolute Moon therefore begins the process towards Belonging.

Truthfully and with love, I thank past listeners and future readers in the islands and the extended African Diaspora. We are not separate, you and I. These essays have come from direct experiences of an island life we share. Their summary in four practical sequences, is the recognition that the value of words is measured through inspired action, discovery, reflection and further action.

May we together create peace within our hearts and by so doing transform our island home into the haven that we long for, as she beckons us unto our collective Belonging to move forward as One, All Mighty, I & I living, seamless, diverse, complete.

1.

Resolute Moon

January

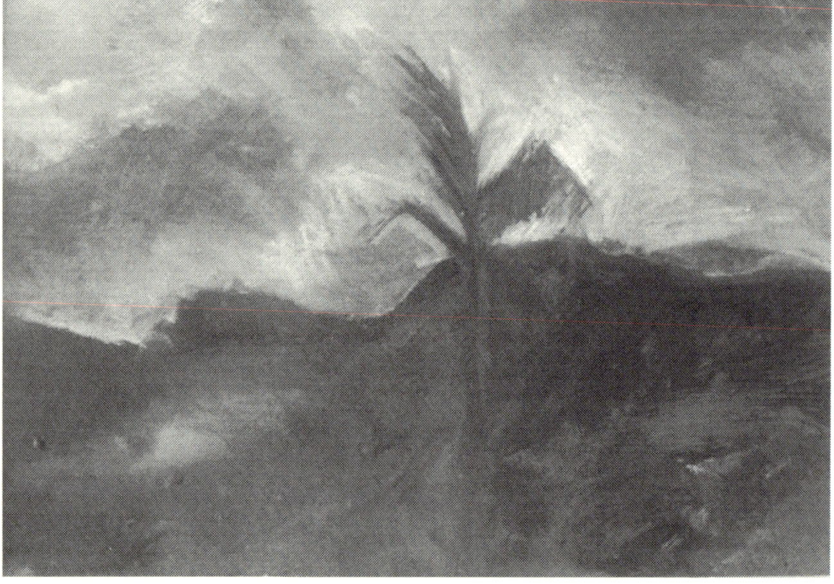

This is the beginning of nature's adventure. It starts with the last days of the returning moon, a continuation; a bridge across the dimensions of life's experience.

Not forced or decorative- simply active in the discovery of the nature's mystery.

Stand firm in her light and we will make the journey together bringing nature's gift into our world. She pleads with us to once again w̶o̶/ manifest her wisdom in our midst.

The Nature of Belonging

Creativity in Daily life

Upon arriving in St. Vincent and the Grenadines in 1992 from my father's birthplace, Trinidad, many things struck me as intriguing enough to adopt the island for long enough to refer to her as 'home'. Having grown up in Africa, been formally educated in England, studied and worked in Japan, Trinidad, and Europe, my subsequent travels took me to Australia, Malaysia, Okinawa, Mexico and many European countries. Yet in 1992, I became engaged to a peculiar little island and her family of sisters.

My intention is not to relate my own personal story, but to illustrate how, against the backdrop of international exposure, a small Caribbean island can captivate the imagination and become a magnetic force to a wandering spirit.

My family in Trinidad were very sceptical about my chosen move. They told me that there was no art or design in St. Vincent and I would never make a living there. It is true that of all the places I had lived and worked, there was, at that time, no evidence of the professional design fields that I had freelanced in previously. But I saw art in other things. I saw it the inherent beauty of the landscape, and in a creative approach to life and survival. I saw it expressed readily in daily lifestyles in rural communities, through productive gardens and other handmade things.

This type of creativity born of necessity reminded me of a genre of beauty revered in Japan called 'wabi', a rustic beauty born of wo/man's intrinsic relationship with their environment through creating things from materials found in the local vicinity. Such forms have practical purpose like the clay oven, the bamboo fence, the wiss (wicker) basket, the trash (thatch) roof. Simple as these things may seem, they have a particular charm and significance that visitors from industrialized societies invariably appreciate. These lowly objects represent freedom from the dependence on machine made goods that govern our lives and, by extension, represent freedom of the individual to create what they need for themselves. The Japanese people have built museums and filled them with wabi artefacts that collectively pronounce the free spirit of natural aesthetic known as 'mingei'- the art of the people.

I recognized the 'wabi' aesthetic in St. Vincent in the character of the then typical Vincentian home. I was struck by the individualism expressed through the vernacular homestead and the variety of materials used in its construction. I noticed that every house was different in design, which I took to reflect the high level of individual creativity of Vincentian people. I later learned that most people had built their own houses, using help from the local community- taking their resourcefulness even further. Each house had a special view in its own customized setting. Creativity, I observed, was expressed through the basic need to provide shelter.

The then typical Vincentian home extended itself into the backyard, an important productive area with kitchen garden; space to potter around and an outdoor laundry area. An essential feature of the homestead was front porch for receiving visitors, interacting with passersby and keeping up with events in the village. Providing space for simple practical aspects of daily life really does seem to impact on quality of life, as the builders of these homes knew. The characterless modular unit or pre-fab type housing visible in many countries, and now being introduced in St. Vincent, does not provide a fertile environment for neighbourly communion. The modular architectural experiment of 1930's Europe culminated in high-rise apartment towers that Ivan Illich, writing in 1980 referred to as places, "where people are stored between trips to the supermarket."[1]

The typical residence of the affluent similarly detracts from neighbourly exchange; their occupants are effectively insulated from the daily smiles and greetings upon which community relations are built.

The then typical Vincentian house not only spoke to me about the creativity of the people but also of the autonomy and freedom born of living close to nature. Having previously researched the origins of mingei first-hand among Japanese rural people, I understood that where the wabi aesthetic manifests, a profound relationship with nature is the artisan's inspiration. The ability to transform natural materials into provision of basic needs, satisfies an eco-psychological yearning, and is the foundation of mental and physical sovereignty. A deep serenity embodied in the consciousness through interaction with nature finds expression in what we make, what we do and what we say. If we detach from her, lack of connection with other human beings is sure to follow.

Little did I realize when I arrived on the island, how quickly what attracted me would begin to disappear from view. In the thirteen years since I arrived, much has changed. I would say the whole focus of life has changed. In those days the emphasis was on providing basic needs of food and shelter, after that one could relax and enjoy community relations (a commonly overlooked requirement for human happiness). The idea of 'basic' needs has shifted to an elaborate house with a lawn replacing the kitchen garden, a car or two, cable TV and various gadgets and fashions to parade our social status. We have become gullible targets for widespread advertising campaigns, which sweep us into the battle (no longer a race) for money to purchase things that ten years ago, before the seductive campaigns targeted us, we would not have thought necessary. The idea of what is 'enough' has expanded considerably, but our means to attain the expanding notion are disproportionately constrained.

The remedy for this situation, creativity through practical problem solving, is no longer culturally prevalent in our daily lives. The need to create has been taken away by inculcated dependence on others termed 'professionals', to provide for us, rather than using our own wit and intelligence. We are aware that the lifestyle we follow is being imported from overseas but that seems to make it all the more desirable. But just as the northern style houses we are now building may suit a temperate climate but are not practical in a tropical one (we would do better to study the principles of design in Caribbean architecture for more comfortable, cooler, energy efficient housing), so too will our 'enough is never enough' attitude prove to be an encumbrance personally, and unsustainable environmentally. In an alarmingly short space of time, we have bought into the idea that we cannot control our own personal space and have become dependent on a stranger to do this for us. The altered aesthetic of what we produce reflects dependency on formulaic solutions as our homes become houses.

As our ability to create resourcefully becomes severely challenged, it is nevertheless, the creative thinker we desperately need to invent appropriate alternatives to the exploitive culture. It is only our creativity that will save us from being perpetual followers of the undesirable aspects of imported cultures.

The mysterious qualities of St. Vincent that enchant the visitor may begin to elude the long-term resident and may never become known to the nationals themselves.

For our own sense of wellbeing and quality of life, our community integrity-not only to attract visitors- we need to rebuild our islands' distinctive character. Their magnetic natural beauty was the creative wellspring that was our past and is our future, made manifest through an observant eye that informs productive hands.

September 2004

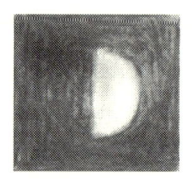

The Cost of Naturalness

One of the most amazing geographical features of the island of St. Vincent, is the proximity of the sea to the rainforest. Her mountainous interior is only several miles from the coast, creating a topographical character found in very few places in the world, even in the Caribbean, where most islands have no rainforest left at all.

By exploring our unspoiled inland areas we can see how the island looked and felt before the rapid commercial development took place. The indigenous inhabitants- the Sibouney, Arawaks and the Garifuna- occupied the island without disturbing its natural order and resources, leaving us a pristine landscape that we have altered drastically through agricultural cultivation and residential development. Yet, despite our obsession with modern development, which marginalizes nature, the sense of nationalism and patriotism is almost always connected to the appreciation of the land in which we live, its natural geographic beauty.

The connection many older Vincentians feel to their homeland is rooted in early memories of country life. They reflect on days gone by when life was definitely not easy but nevertheless uncomplicated and safe. People lived lives that were more self-reliant and needs were met within the community. Only a matter of years ago, we lived so closely to nature that it is amazing to think that there is now a generation of under 25-year-olds for whom TV culture is a reality and who seek artificial means for mental stimulation rather than an interaction with nature.

What is very obvious when we hike into the unspoilt interior of the island, is the peace and power of nature. The songs of the birds, of water in the streams, are pure sounds, rhythmic and harmonious. Behind the tranquillity, a complex intelligence of nature resides. Any farmer who works in the mountains will tell you that nature is a marvellous and awesome force by whose kind permission we survive on her bounty of water, earth and air. Coming down from the mountain into villages, the sounds change as we detect the presence of human life and community. In the rural areas, nature is incorporated into daily life through farming and kitchen gardens that supply vegetables for the household. The old houses are oriented to keep cool and porches face the roadside so residents and passers by interact freely. In this traditional community setting, people live side by side with nature.

Closer to the city in the residential areas such as Arnos Vale, Montrose, Cane Garden and Dorsetshire Hill, residents have moved in from other areas and modern communities have sprung up. In these residences, nature is left further behind- gardens are manicured and decorative, lawns are fashionable and plants live in neatly arranged pots. Houses compete for grandeur and nature resides there as a decorative accessory. The inhabitants are rarely seen outside the house, porches are usually behind the house, doors and windows are closed, and the houses appear empty, devoid of life. Moving into the city itself and all signs of nature have gone; the last piece of greenery in the town centre was destroyed by the construction of the Central Market several years ago. Every mature tree in town has been ruthlessly cut down. From here in the city, the mountain background seems like another world, nature is excluded totally from town culture.

The journey we have taken from mountain to city has revealed subcultures within our societies that are characterized by how closely they live with nature: in the mountain; in the rural community; the residential areas or the suburbs; the urban or city environment. These distinct social groups have different lifestyles and customs and separation between them has come about as the common connection with nature disappears.

The more affluent people become, the less they have to do with other social groups and this disconnection turns into insulation which in turn becomes dislike, and even fear of, other social groups. In this way, society has broken down as modern development compromises nature and community. Because of the lengthy separation and eventual divorce from nature, we face difficult times ahead. Reconciliation does not lie in our quest for affluence, (which is really a state where we lose sight of what is 'enough') which suppresses our true nature.

But reconciliation with nature will inevitably come, as evidence from all over the world shows that to survive an energy crisis and increasing man made and natural disasters, we will have to live once again closer to nature, and utilize her sustainably. When we eventually turn to her for assistance, we will ask, "Why did we move so far away? Why did we destroy so much? Why did we not teach our children to live and work with nature? Why did we turn our backs on our landscape?" And our ancestors, who lived for centuries without disturbing nature's complex intelligence, serving their communities first, will be recognized as having infinitely more wisdom than modern man.

Artist Paul Klee summed up a profound observation in one sentence when he wrote:

> "There is no need to disparage the joy of novelty; though a clear view of history should save us from desperately searching for novelty at the cost of naturalness."[2]

December 2004

The Seeds of Culture

The word 'culture' is one often heard in Caribbean islands and has narrowly come to mean 'entertainment'. In scientific or biological terms a culture is a group of organisms that are cultivated or grown in prescribed conditions favourable to the culture's growth.

'Cultivate', the action word that relates to culture, denotes encouraging growth or expansion of something. The word 'cultivate' was originally used to refer to farming crops, but it also means to improve or develop something by study or education, to educate a person or group. In this sense, cultural education is to do with the growth and expansion of the whole child or person.

However, 'culture' as we often use the word in the Caribbean, refers to 'performance', 'show' or 'entertainment'; sometimes of traditional style, and most often associated with a tourist attraction. The constant use of this limited interpretation has redefined what culture means to us as a people; it has classified 'culture' as a preoccupation of tourists and the affluent, giving way to the notion that ordinary people don't have culture, that they are in fact 'uncultured'. But such an assumption is wholly inappropriate because the island culture we can claim as authentically 'Vincy' is agri-culture: the practice of growing things and understanding the conditions to make them grow; an action, which reflects the true meaning of the word 'culture'.

Our farmers and people in rural communities are, in this sense, bona fide caretakers and generators of culture. Farming has been, and still is, the dominant way of life for many Vincentian (although the empirical origins of this culture have been adulterated by applied theory). Interestingly, culture as agriculture has not been seriously considered as a viable alternative tourism product based on indigenous culture, despite the fact that the fastest growing niche tourism products globally are those of rural and agri-tourism.

In our haste to duplicate a commercialized tourism product, we have developed a new meaning of the word culture: sporadic entertainment as a momentary escape from life's routine. But a society's culture is much more than this. It's an evolving intangible experience fed through the senses of living beings, everyday customs and habits; what people eat, how they speak, what they grow, how they go about their daily lives, and how they feel about all they do.

The production of glossy cultural packages has redefined the cultural experience and removed it from daily life. Community culture lacks lustre by comparison and is frowned upon as something to eradicate, leaving the practice of agriculture to languish taking up a lowly position on the ladder of social occupation. Its true worth as scientific enterprise is not even considered worthy of schools' curricula. As investigation of any historic civilization will bear out, authentic culture is cultivated through awareness of its value, and in order to grow strong, healthy roots are a necessity. Our predominant modern culture, has its roots overseas, having been imported from industrialized countries. We can't lay true claim to this second-hand culture that renders us copyists. It doesn't dig itself into the substance of island creativity. We cannot build an authentic civilization on a rootless second-hand culture.

The forms of expression that the rural communities have generated from their relationship with the earth have been marginalized by a top heavy, second-hand culture. Cultural proximity with the land only exists now within an ageing sector of the population and accordingly our understanding of natural elements depreciates as we seek to control and dominate nature rather than work along with her. Trinidadian writer Earl Lovelace says of people in farming communities:

"These are people I have tremendous respect for and I believe that in the village and in the countryside these people are the salt of the earth- what they have maintained is very important for us.

"I am saying to those of you who live in the country that you do not have to feel inferior to anybody, that you do not have to hanker after the baubles and the bright lights of the city. You should feel solidified by the culture that you have among you, before you seek to give it over for something else."[3]

Lovelace implores country people to be proud of what they have, even though they may see others trying to escape from it, forsaking it for a form of development that robs them of their own culture.

As a society we treat the earth and agriculture, the art and science of the soil, as something to be cleared away, not something upon which our future rests. And, in chasing the values of industrial city life where people rarely touch the earth, or dip their toes in the sea, we must weep for our islands whose beauty is no longer something that we connect with to create appropriate cultural forms. The first step to reclaiming an authentic culture is becoming aware of the natural environment and how to take care of it, then how to harness it for our needs sustainably with appropriate technology. This understanding is the aim of cultural education and upon its foundation, we can create authentic forms, whether through cooking a meal, starting a business, painting a picture, building a house, producing alternative energy systems, or designing a tourism product. An endogenous cultural identity is an economic asset to be cultivated before the seeds disappear forever.

February 2005

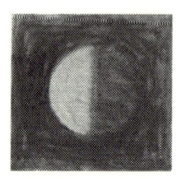

Purposeful Resolutions

'Resolute' is how we often start the year; having identified some aspects of our lives that need improvement, we resolve to attend to them purposefully. The resolutions may be short lived as we veer off course shifting our priorities from inner resolve to outer influence. As the upstanding nature of resolve is corrupted in this annual manner, its virtues of determination, practical action and purposefulness necessary to vital accomplishment, may also be undermined in the process. Perhaps if we were to recognize resolution as an outcome of 'resolute undertaking', rather than as a promise we make to ourselves, we would accomplish discernible goals instead of giving up in the face of distraction.

Many grass root projects across the globe make fascinating study of resolute action. The determination and purposefulness demonstrated in these global initiatives, is part of a conscious movement that has as its goal, flourishing synergies between the natural environment and sustainable human enterprise. Human creativity is seen as the catalyst for resolute action that provides practical solutions to socio-economic problems.

The outstanding efforts of 2006 Nobel Peace Prize laureate, Muhammed Yunus, developed one of these compelling poverty solutions called 'micro-franchising'; a global initiative that involves the creation of networks of small, successful, locally-owned businesses, designed for replication, providing essential goods and service plus jobs in low-income communities. The activities of the Grameen Bank grew from an encounter in a street in Bangladesh between Mr. Yunus and some desperately poor people who were in debt. He empathized with them and lent them the money to pay off their debt which was 27 US dollars. He found their lives were transformed by this gesture, enabling them to become productive. The moral compensation for him was immense and spurred him on to do the same for more people. The mission of Mr. Yunus' Grameen Bank is now to empower the world's poorest people to lift themselves out of poverty with dignity. With tiny loans, financial services and technology, they help the poor, mostly women, to start sustainable businesses. Within less than ten years of being founded in Bangladesh, the bank's global network of microfinance partners has reached nearly 3 million families in 22 countries.

The BBC's World Challenge competition highlights and rewards similar examples of community enterprise and innovation. Some of these businesses employ 500 families, such as the one in Indonesia that developed coconut matting to prevent land erosion. The 2006 winner was a Sri Lankan enterprise that makes paper out of elephant dung. Apart from producing a quality product, and creating employment, this project has saved the lives of elephants, because farmers, who used to kill them, now earn money from selling the dung for papermaking.

There are many such examples of grassroots projects designed for micro-enterprise in developing countries, that focus on the ability of small people-based projects to tackle larger issues of poverty and economic development. It's important to note that none of these successful projects was government initiated: all were founded on the resolute action of ordinary individuals. So this begs the question- if one man with a small group of friends can affect the lives of nearly 3 million families in 22 countries, what extraordinary feats are we capable of in our tiny island communities? The grassroots projects demonstrate that meaningful progress starts with self-organization and an attitude of social responsibility. But the key factor in every successful micro-enterprise is the application of problem-solving skills to engender practical outcomes.

The Nature of Belonging

Looking at these examples one could conclude that empowerment lies in the direct manipulation of one's immediate environment to bring about improvement to economic circumstances. We also learn from these worldwide examples that meaningful progress impacting positively on poor people's lives, does not start with impressive visible structures. It can start in someone's backyard, on a porch, in a kitchen, with a conversation between two people, and utilizes what is available in the vicinity.

We can take the observation of progress being based our actions and thoughts even further- where it begins entirely without physical structure, without organization or government, but within our own minds and interaction; with meaningful dialogue.

Dialogue is exchange between two or more parties that results in mutual understanding and acceptance. From my observation, the most important part of this process is listening with the genuine intention to understand another's perspective without projecting our own opinions onto it. Dialogue in this sense is something we don't engage in very often (maybe we don't have time?) and would do well to resolve to do better. It takes practice to cultivate openness and receptivity to prevail over sudden reaction, instant conclusions or judgments. It involves consideration of viewpoint different from our own so that we can hold many contrasting possibilities in our mind simultaneously. Physicist David Bohm has suggested that an inability to dialogue effectively is the cause of our social crises and that if we practice this type of dialogue, "the whole structure of defence and attack can collapse and change to one of participation and sharing." The sharing consciousness is absolutely necessary, Bohm suggests, for society not to fall apart. With reference to the role that dialogue can play in existing organizations, Bohm, Donald Factor and Peter Garrett establish that, "The spirit of Dialogue is one of free play, a sort of collective dance of mind that, nevertheless, has immense power and reveals coherent purpose. Once begun it becomes continuing adventure that can open the way to significant and creative change."[4]

At this point we can easily grasp the notion of dialogue as fundamental to progress- if, without meaningful dialogue society falls apart, then dialogue must be vital to meaningful progress. It stands to reason then, that progress rests on the qualities necessary for dialogue which are an open receptive mind; a willingness to listen and, of course, empathy. Such dialogue has resulted in sustainable solutions to social and economic problems as we have seen in the example of micro-finance. Had Mr. Yunus not been able to empathize, the Grameen Bank would never have started and flourished. Mr. Yunus' project, and those in the World Challenge competition, began with simple dialogue in real situations based on listening and questioning, and developed from small beginnings to provide sustainable solutions to widespread social and economic problems.

So how could our communities benefit from such dialogue and why do we not engage in it more often? The answer may be because obstruction to meaningful dialogue is built into our daily lives. It has become part of our culture and could be our main constraint to sustainable development. Obstructions to dialogue prevent us from being heard, something we all experience in the form of entrenched positions and prejudices of the 'isms': sexism, racism, class snobbism, elitism, authoritarianism, political 'partisanism'. The belief that one religion is better than another; perceiving oneself to be more 'spiritual' and closer to God than another also obstructs empathetic communion, as does the authoritarian view that we are superior because of our position- elected, official, uniformed or self-appointed. All these attitudes abandon the necessity to listen effectively and are thus obstacles to meaningful dialogue. If, in expounding our beliefs, we expect others to agree with us without listening to their perspective, we are directly responsible for obstructing understanding and progress through meaningful dialogue.

The Nature of Belonging

The variety of effective 'isms' were selected and strategically placed in island societies to subordinate the majority. We have endured a repressive colonial history where dialogue was never encouraged. Vincentian Ann-Marie John wrote in her important article in the Searchlight newspaper, "the exercise of free speech is a defining feature for the growth and prosperity of any free and rights' conscious society."[5]

Whilst freedom of speech is essential to meaningful dialogue, free speech without listening does not create dialogue.

Examples of obstacles to daily dialogue abound, some broadcast to the nation in 'interactive' radio programmes, when a caller is hastily judged as either in agreement or disagreement with the moderator, rather than as a contributor whose experience sheds another important facet onto the topic being discussed. Though they do not demonstrate participatory discussion, these programmes do provide informative listening to the cultural analyst researching socially acceptable discriminatory practices, but they cannot be termed 'socially empowering'. Dialogue is not cultivated in an environment where the emphasis is only on canvassing agreement. Communication practiced without the skill of listening, excludes validation of the views and experiences of others.

The fact that we can change the world by listening with empathy has been demonstrated by Nobel Peace Prize laureate Muhammed Yunus' micro-financing initiative. With so much in our beloved St Vincent and the Grenadines that we would love to change for the better, did we ever imagine a transformation could be so close at hand, within our own listening minds and conversations?

A new year, a new moon, and every revolution of the planet from dawn to pre-dawn holds the promise of regeneration, progress and resolution. Could listening with empathy become a desirable habit that we resolutely attend to as an intangible requisite for a productive society? As a process that grows from within, could this simple resolution enhance micro- enterprise and local economy more effectively than the official structures built to do the same?

December 2006

Message from the Resolute Moon

Through direct observation, we consolidate our relationship with nature, empowering her to engage us in meaningful relationship through productivity appropriate to purpose.

> *Such action can liberate
> those who, without a voice,
> have never been heard.*

2.

Ancestral Moon

February

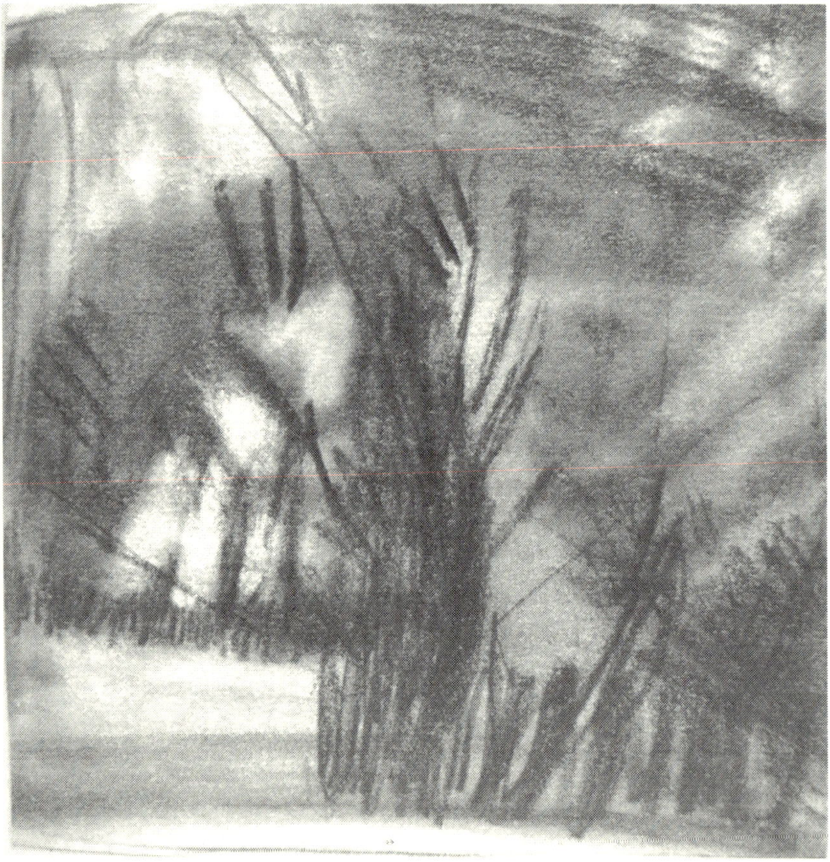

*In days gone by drawings had magical power- images were mystic explorations,
spiritual journeys;*

landscapes were not only to have material existence but also to reach out into the realm of Immortality.

The Impulse of Black History

Throughout the African Diaspora, February is designated 'Black History Month.' In St. Vincent and the Grenadines, this is the month when we have commentaries in the newspapers and lectures addressing different aspects of African culture and heritage in the context of the Caribbean experience. The Afrikan Heritage Foundation, Rastafari Working Committee and the Inivershall Rastafari Movement collaborate to bring us films, lectures, and discussions to educate us about our African ancestry. Many small islanders may question the importance of such an education, yet interestingly, they may not challenge those researching their Scottish, English or European ancestry. This demonstrates the prevailing Eurocentric attitude, even though European settlers historically formed a minority of the island population.

The annually disseminated information about Black History has focused on the presence of Africans, called the Garifuna, on Caribbean islands before Columbus arrived, and we have been told about the migration of Africans throughout all continents of the world, hundreds of years before the European colonies were established. Archaeological discoveries documented in numerous books and academic research papers, reveal that the African civilization of ancient Kemet was far more advanced than European historical sources would have us believe, and that the European version of history omitted the truth to serve their interests in the exploitation of Africans throughout the colonial era.

Despite the archaeological findings of our own Dr. Earl Kirby and the partial documentation of his immense knowledge

The Nature of Belonging

born of a lifetime's work that could enlighten us academically and spiritually, we know very little about how the culture of Africa is woven into our own. With regard to our awareness of our African ancestry and identification with African heritage, the tools of colonization have been highly effective in uprooting the collective psyche from its origins. The majority of Afro-Caribbean people identify materially and spiritually more readily with European and American cultures than those of Africa. This psychic displacement has come about not only through enforcement before Independence, but also since then through prescribed development policies, systematic education, and the negative impact of the tourism industry.

Somehow, though, a modicum of African consciousness has survived and we now have distinct camps of Afro-Caribbean people on the islands and in the Diaspora, who either connect with their African heritage or do not. There are those who, influenced by the civil rights and Black Power movements of the 1960s and 70s, and the Rastafari movement from Jamaica, will acknowledge their African heritage with pride and possession.

But many others, through mainstream social conditioning, seem oblivious to, or even ashamed of, our African lineage.

The authentic African cultural aesthetic appears to have been practically eradicated from the surface of the small island. Like its Asian Indian counterpart, it hangs precariously over a precipice where ethnophobics venture to sever the last tenuous threads and launch it to its ultimate fate beneath the earth. But in their ignorance they are sending it back from whence it came, deep within the earth that nurtured it and where it gathers strength to resurface. The attempt to destroy the ethno-aesthetic is futile for another reason: whilst not consciously demonstrated, it is the ancestral force at work through the movements and latent abilities of its inheritors. John Stewart in his address at the CARIFESTA Symposia 1992 said that, "The word 'aesthetic', although commonly associated with art, really addresses a need and form of practice that is as universal amongst us as biological hunger or the submission to sleep."[6]

In this statement Stewart implies that the aesthetic is a basic need that was once fulfilled through daily practice of making things, ritual and community enactment. All of these were central to African culture, but all were suppressed under colonialism. We see the aesthetic tenuously preserved in traditional African artforms, in J'ouvert mas', in Spiritual Baptism; an aesthetic that once forged a powerful connection of the community to nature and spirit. African spirituality, like indigenous religions throughout the world, invested life and meaning into every tree, stone, mountain and person. Their art forms resonate infusion with character and expression. In our islands, at present, pictorial images are validated as 'artistic' only in so far as they duplicate the photo-realistic style that originated in Europe. Since the invention of the camera, European artists of the impressionist movement, inspired by African and oriental art, began the movement towards a more expressive pictorial reality over a hundred years ago.

It seems we are caught in a cultural time warp, one which some of the younger generation are beginning to break out of, though not without a great struggle ahead of them. They will instigate a step towards authentic expression because they are the ones most frustrated by a sense of cultural conflict experienced by many Afro-Caribbean people. The spirit of African heritage is strong and unbreakable in our music, voices and posture, in the patterns and rhythms of language and expression. Having worked with them, I bear witness to the overwhelming force of creative expression within the youth and I see it, in some cases, crushed by compliance to mass conformity.

The daily struggle many of our artists endure is a struggle against the dominance of Eurocentric values and the negation of the creative spirit of the people. It's a struggle against forces that oppose cultural diversity. It's a struggle of cultural tensions in the society, between free expression and hierarchical suppression. The intuitive expression/spirit/ aesthetic is oppressed through

The Nature of Belonging

deliberately orchestrated channels, as Caribbean writer Lloyd Best implied when he said in a CARIFESTA Symposium in 1994:

" And how, I ask you, are we to make those vital connections with our native tradition, with the tradition of ourselves, if we did not invoke the statement of the artist? If we did not give free reign to our poetic sensibility, terrorized as it has been by its institutionalized setting?"[7]

It is for the artists and other cultural creatives to articulate the destructive elements of oppressive culture: consumerism; eradication of nature through profit-driven development; the culture of judgmental hierarchies that suppress women, the youth and the poor.

Will the information disseminated in Black History month impact on the consciousness of the general public to contemplate these critical questions? To what extent will it bring the realization that cultural history is not only to be grasped intellectually but essentially through action, experience and interaction in daily life? How can knowledge of historical facts incite us to reclaim the culture of expression, let it grow stronger through our youth and quell the atmosphere of fear and intimidation that is only possible because we are not aware of our own strength? How can we anchor the knowledge to prevent our youth from drifting?

The rhythms of African culture have receded on the surface of this modern day society, but they still reside within the life and breath of our children. It is in their passion, in their responses and in their energy. They are born with their heritage intact within them, like earthlings on the moon. Unless this genetic impulse is validated and channelled, surely Black History Month comes and goes like any other month, clearly demonstrating how issues of collective cultural importance are put into words but not into our hearts or actions.

February 2007

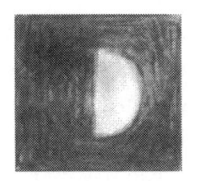

Inheriting Wisdom of the Youth

The struggle of historical revolutionary movements has been for liberation from oppressive regimes. The cloud of enslavement casts a dark shadow over the entire historic story of Africa's descendants and the survival of their culture in the African Diaspora.

Garifuna Chief, Joseph Chatoyer, was elevated to the status of the National Hero of St. Vincent and the Grenadines because he led his people into battle for freedom by continuing a 200-year-old war against would-be-oppressors. Freedom, as perceived in the West, is 'freedom of the individual to choose', but I would suggest that the freedom the Chatoyer's people, the Garifuna, fought for, was for preservation of an indigenous culture that was not based on individual personality and ambition but on the interconnectedness of community.

We have many examples within the culture of individualism in small island societies that people are not liberated, and cannot act or follow through with even those actions that are for the collective good. Many community groups with the best intentions fail through sabotage. Altruism is viewed suspiciously and individual initiative can be paralysed in a culture of individuality. From personal observation and experience, I would postulate that freedom of a people is attained through employing their energies collectively for the good of their mental, physical and spiritual wellbeing. This state of freedom cannot be realized through words alone that say 'we are free', because words cannot grant its attainment- action and interaction must take place for it to become a sate of being.

The Nature of Belonging

We may express ourselves freely in words, but if our efforts to act for the greater good are thwarted, then we are not free. In this sense, by educating our children to cooperate with eachother in meaningful activity based on their own ideas, through creative education, we are educating them to be free. If freedom to act for the greater good is the true nature of freedom, then there are a lot of people in our society still in captivity. There are many whose actions do not impact positively on others, but create a state of mental and emotional confinement and dependence for themselves and others.

Individual freedom may create an illusion of freedom in the guise of multiple choices that are money driven: what clothes to buy; what car to drive; how big a house to build; the most lucrative profession to choose; what drugs to take; how many sexual partners to entertain. Contrary to freedom based on the greater good, individual freedom of choice can be detrimental to self and others.

In celebrating Black History month, which should uplift us collectively as a proud people, we could consciously ask ourselves if we are acting in liberating proactive ways, or if we have ushered further imposition into our lives. Many children and youth are imposed upon to constrain their own thoughts and actions, bombarded with the culture of multiple choice and the frustration of underachievement that has been assigned to them. If Black History and Emancipation mean anything to us, let us honour the centuries old struggle for liberation through granting freedom of action to our youth: encourage them to engage and enquire, to question and formulate ideas; to expand from limitation; to feel free in their own inheritance, the majesty of our islands, for then they will love where they are, love their communities and families, connect with their islands; heal themselves from the trauma of emotional and physical abuse and transform the negativity poured upon them into positive action and respect. They will feel the privilege of life itself -not as individual inheritance of choices- but as a gift of compassion to be used for the greater good.

This is where I hope the journey of Black History will carry us- a voyage that is fraught with struggle but one that we can steer towards brighter days out of the captivity of our own prejudices and negative attitudes, permanently dispersing the cloud of enslavement that has overcast our greatness.

Shemon Baptiste, as a college student feeling the weight of persecution for being young, bright and creative, given the freedom to express herself wrote: "The steps we take together mean more than the steps we take apart."[8] Her statement wisely recognizes the value of community culture over competitive individualism. In following her advice, let us take steps with our children and youths to learn from the wisdom they are capable of, if they are listened to and encouraged to act according to their own nature as living creative beings. In such spirited action, their contribution to the nation will be immeasurable in rebuilding the community culture that Paramount Chief Chatoyer fought so bravely to preserve.

February 2009

In the Hundreds

There is a cluster of villages in 'The Valley of Longevity' in Ecuador, South America where people live to be well over a hundred years old. Researchers have been astonished to find that these old people, ranging in age from 100 to 140 years, read without glasses and can do intricate manual tasks such as playing guitar and dressing themselves.

They live in small self-sufficient farming communities with extended family spanning three or four generations. At age ninety, they retire from digging the land and take on lighter tasks such as herding goats, harvesting crops and planting. They farm without chemical fertilizers and their diet is fairly basic: corn porridge, bush tea, goat's milk and meat once or twice a week. Alcohol is consumed, but not on a daily basis. Walking around their mountainous farms provides them with plenty of exercise.

But these are not an especially resilient strain of human being- as soon as they move to towns, or urban areas, they succumb to heart disease and cancer like the average population and their life expectancy falls to the common average of 75 years. The difference between rural life and city or urban life, is made clear here in terms of physical endurance. The lifestyle in towns and residential areas impact the mind and body differently compared to that in a rural community. The detrimental effects to health predominately occur through diet, exercise and stress levels associated with a faster pace of life. In such a small island as ours, this contrast of lifestyle is obvious. We need no facts- as useful as they are- because we can glean from direct observation and personal experience, that changes in our shape and agility accords with our dietary habits.

We can observe from local newspaper photographs of our own centenarians, that these living treasures are usually slight in frame; they have told us that their diet was mainly naturally grown fruits, vegetables and ground provisions. Our bodies thrive on and relish natural local produce, but the taste buds on our tongues seem to have more say in what we choose to eat. The transfer of control of our health from body to head mirrors the shift from the gutsy rural communities to the heady city or settlements overseas. In taking an 'upward' step, we are actually adopting a new lifestyle that is not conducive to holistic health.

Our sister windward isle Dominica, has three times the average incidence of centenarians than developed countries such as Britain and the United States and, like the Valley of Longevity, has attracted the interest of researchers. Dr Noel Boaz, an American professor of anatomy at the Ross Medical School in Dominica states,

> "the key to their longevity is diet and lifestyle, not genetics. Dominica is a mountainous island with its interior cloaked in dense rainforest. Roads were few until well into the 1960s, so when today's elderly were young, long distance walking on rough terrain was a necessity of everyday life, along with hard physical work. Their diet would have included natural products from the forest, herbs and herbal medicines, as well as that rich diversity of cultivated fruit and vegetables, almost all of it grown in their own gardens."[9]

In 2004, BBC correspondent John Pickford traveled to Dominica to discover why some Dominicans live longer than people elsewhere. When he met 102-year-old Rudolph Edward Georges, Pickford was surprised "with the strength of his handshake".[10] Mr Georges told him "everything I planted I ate

The Nature of Belonging

and everything I ate I planted". Like many of our farmer elders, he produced his own cocoa, had his own chickens, goats and a cow and did the work on his smallholding after the long trek back from his job on a tobacco plantation. His 'Sunday special' was a glass of strong beer mixed with milk, eggs and sugar, plus a dash of lime and nutmeg which must have guaranteed physical fortitude, as at ninety-eight years old Mr Georges travelled unaccompanied to England to visit one of his sons.

But according to Dr Boaz, the centenarian phenomenon will not more than another decade: "Two American-style fast-food restaurants have recently opened in Roseau. There are TVs in even the poorest households, car ownership has risen to one in four of the population and working on the land is a last choice job for the young."

The centenarians eating a traditional diet, drinking bush tea and taking plenty of exercise will testify that a natural peaceful collaboration with the body is far more productive in terms of years alive than imposing an artificial chemical war on it with fast food.

The era the centenarians lived through is coming to an end. As farmland disappears, our diets change to processed food; living expenses escalate to support the modern lifestyle and inevitable medical expenses as our health deteriorates. The centenarians are surely wise ones, whose knowledge cannot be passed on unless we listen to them.

I for one, feel blessed, not only because my grandparents were Dominican, but because I eat what I grow from my garden and that I can visit a treasured elder of Vermont, Lawrence "Captain" Guy who at the age of almost ninety years, has initiated an organic farming project. If we listen to the wisdom of our elders, we'd learn that simple pleasures, easily within reach, are key to long productive lives that should be the norm rather than the exception.

In Ecuador, modernization has caused the numbers of centenarians to drop from twelve in 2000, to five in 2006. The reason, according to the town's health clinic doctor, "is a decline in healthy conditions caused by increasing modernization. People lived an extremely quiet, conservative way of life. They went to bed early and ate only what they produced, all natural with no pesticides or fertilizers. Now those habits and tranquility have changed: junk food has replaced the grains and the discotheques the tranquility."

We can surely see our own reflection in these places that once practiced the earthy lifestyle of our elders. It is the choice of a modern culture to lust after novelty and shorten lives in the process, but can we provide healthier options for more conscious future generations? Can we ensure that there will at least be nourishing food for them to eat, springs to water them, clean rivers to bathe in, enough trees to generate oxygen and places to walk safely? As a traditional way of life disappears, does the alternative that beckons provide a better (albeit shorter) life?

February 2007

Plot to Freedom

Cultural events such as lectures, poetry readings, music and dance performances all play an important role in teaching us about our history and cultural identity. Our artists, historians, the poets, writers and musicians keep culture alive and must support each other as custodians and promoters of national culture. Yet, there's a vital aspect of culture that kept our ancestors alive and created our heritage, that is, the practice of growing food.

In the race to become modernized, this practice, once a central focus of life, is now barely visible in our communities. Yet not so long ago, each family grew all the food they needed and exchanged surplus within the community. The knowledge that came with this practice amounts to a national treasure of proportions that few understand. Self-reliant sustainable agri-culture, also grew integrated communities and gave rise to a myriad of authentic Caribbean cultural forms.

Picture, if you can, the scene on a typical plantation where slaves were forced to work in the fields fourteen hours per day, six days per week. They had but one day each week to provide their own food from a small cultivation plot called a 'provision plot', 'freedom plot' or 'yam piece'. It not only provided food, but became a place where the enslaved were free to be themselves and to act creatively without authority figures watching over them. The plots were strenuous to access, as the best land was reserved for the estate crops, and the farming methods employed there were different from those on the cane or cotton plantation.

The provision plots became carriers of indigenous culture and knowledge passed down from generation to generation.

The same plot was endlessly productive without constant relocation or artificial fertilizers, hosting a healthy mixture of plants, vegetables, medicinal herbs, fruit trees and root crops. Our fore-parents intuitively practiced rotation cropping. They had a cattle patch that supplied natural fertilizer and made functional objects from many of the raw materials. On the long walks to the plot they told stories, sang songs and rhythms while they worked. These plots of land, the source of their physical and mental health, became centres of African cultural preservation.

An indigenous communal culture was built up and passed on in the provision plot throughout the most prolonged period of inhuman suffering throughout world history.

The freedom plot and its descendant, the humble kitchen garden, was created and maintained through close observation and understanding of nature, using the same principles of natural farming that modern agriculturalists in the industrialized world term 'agroforestry', 'permaculture', or 'forest gardening'. But centuries before these systems were introduced in the west, our fore-parents had developed an energy-efficient sustainable system of food production that supplied whole families from only one day's work per week.

These plots sustained Caribbean communities and later expanded into the lucrative provision export market known in the islands as 'trafficking'. The story of the freedom plot is one of creativity, resourcefulness, community building and commerce. It is a story about a culture that survived intact beneath the force of oppression. In "We want to Become Wise", Oscar Allen writes: "The freedom plot was like another life with African crops, African work ways, African market skills and management and mobility and socializing. Under all of that the provision plot promised to be the land of the future. The provision plot was a seed that would outgrow the plantation."

Educating ourselves about historical events should lead us to an understanding of how our survival was made possible by the working of the provision plot. In acknowledging Independence,

The Nature of Belonging

Emancipation, Black History, we empathize with the efforts of communities from whom we have descended and understand how they cultivated community values whilst trapped in the plantation system and monetary poverty. It is the most amazing cultural phenomenon that, despite the conditions of enslavement, a rich African heritage was preserved through working the freedom plot.

We may salute individual heroes in positions of leadership, but their accomplishments are founded on the mental and physical endurance of the communities that reared them.

The idea that freedom and a deep understanding of our culture lies within the soil is at odds with the squeaky-clean, hands off culture we've accepted from England and America. We now value lawns and decorative landscaping more than the food productive garden. Those who sustained our survival without fanfare, who carry the remnants of noble culture, who have the knowledge that our youth need to save the land, pass on neglected, stigmatized, even themselves conditioned to believe that an educated professional with no cultural awareness or understanding, is superior to a humble person of the soil and community.

Within the context of educating ourselves on matters of island culture and history, I would argue that the humble gardener/provider was not only a custodian of a precious heritage but also a cultural revolutionary, for within their world of natural cultivation, they kept the vision and action of freedom alive for their descendants to make reality.

The freedom plot *did* outgrow the plantation, but it succumbed to another form of imperialism- globalized consumer culture.

A legacy where a fraction of the population could feed everyone else with one day's labour per week and have surplus for trade, is surely the most valuable of cultural forms well worth preserving and one that harbours important lessons. As in the past, once again in the future, the art of resourcefulness is sure to be our only means of survival.

March 2008

Message from the Ancestral Moon

The historical experience of our people enlightens us on the meaning of liberation as it was lived and can be lived again. Cultural sovereignty through the art of harvesting with dignity and respect for the earth, produced National Heroes and Elders to live long in our midst so we could become wise in theirs.

3.
Birthing Moon

March

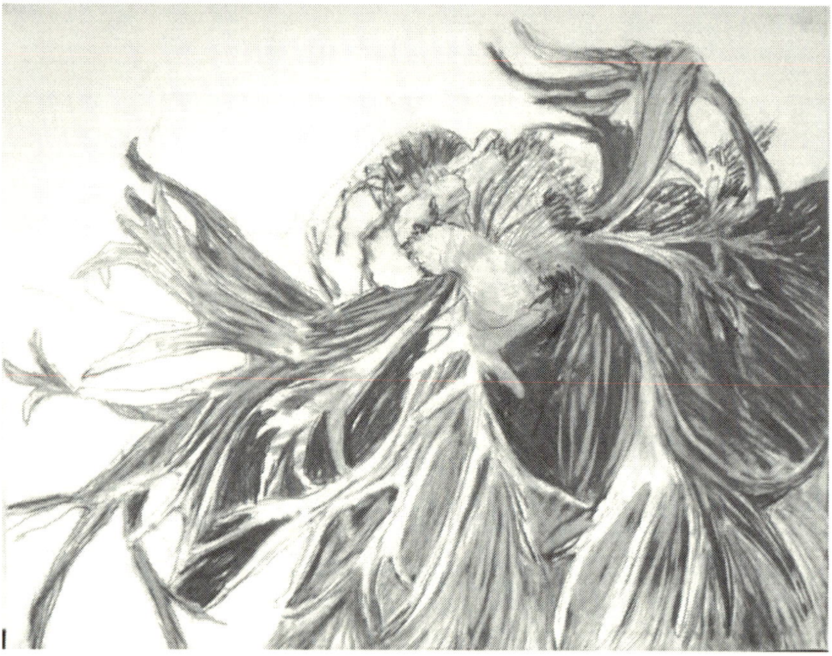

*Thought dispersed the cloud that before was being.
Live as the light lives!*

National Hero or Dangerous Revolutionary?

If we are curious about why Emancipation Day, National Heroes Day, African Liberation Day and Independence, are holidays in our yearly calendar, we can read our newspaper columns and other sources of information and discover that they stem from activities associated with civil rights' movements, political milestones, campaigns and social activism that mobilized around acknowledgement of the fundamental right to freedom.

This is what we assume St. Vincent's national hero Paramount Chief Joseph Chatoyer, fought for but freedom for and from what?

As his community had no access to manufactured goods and other properties of capitalist society, their experience of freedom must have been very different to ours. As such, we can assume that what Chief Chatoyer committed to securing for his people was freedom from outside influence and the right to self-government; sovereignty was sought through the right to occupy land that his communities and previous generations resided upon.

It is evident through analysis of the society's aesthetic tradition, that the Garifuna people perceived the land, culture, and survival as interdependent. The forest and sea sustained them; their possessions and customs reflected their relationship with nature. They belonged to the land, not the other way round. Deprivation of relationship with the natural environment and loss of liberty were one and the same in this freedom as it was lived by the Garifuna.

The Nature of Belonging

It's important for us to grasp this in order to understand, through comparison, what freedom means to us today. It certainly does not depend on our relationship with the land. For the majority, that connection has been severed completely. So is freedom for us being able to choose the way we live, to do what we want, to express ourselves, or having enough money to buy anything we want? Many of us feel captive in the system of social pigeonholing that assigns us modern day roles. We may feel that freedom lies in getting more money to escape such captivity. But once our basic needs are met, asset accumulation, and its partner, debt, are themselves trappings that do not alleviate our neuroses. Fear of what others think about us, expectations placed upon us by family, peers and colleagues can also negatively impact our sense of freedom, trapping us in mental dependency.

So what is freedom to us?

What ever it is, it does not qualify as the freedom that Chief Chatoyer fought for – collective responsibility and the right to maintain a cohesive (ecologically sustainable) community. So then why would we uphold such a role model to the nation when our concept of freedom is something different? What is the precise meaning of the events and holidays that we take time off work for?

I cannot tell you what life among the Kalinago or Garifuna was like, but I can go into the rainforest and see what they saw, breathe in the special fusion of air and shadow between the trees, contemplate the sun rise and sunset, listen to the birdsong, treasure the rainbows in the valleys, and know that they who fought for freedom, heard, saw and felt all these. This is what they fought for- the natural living world and their tangible connection with it. How puzzling, then, that we should applaud Chatoyer's battle annually when consideration for the life-giving qualities that he fought for, is absent from our mainstream culture. We must ask ourselves why is he our hero? Are we idolizing a sentimental image? We live in conflict with the values held by his society as we have colonized nature into a servant subordinating to our controlling minds, taking what we need. Whilst her resources diminish, we thrive. Is this what freedom is?

If our national hero came back today would he be given a hero's welcome with air-time on the TV and radio, or would he be labelled a crazy dreamer? If he mustered forces to fight for his community values wouldn't he be branded a dangerous terrorist? Wouldn't his actions and way of life be opposed today as disruptive and inconsistent with modern development? No doubt this rationale was exactly what the British used to annihilate him and his community culture. Are we not then being hypocritical in upholding him whilst taking the stance of those who orchestrated his downfall?

I suggest that if we think seriously about Chief Chatoyer's legacy, it may lead us to confront our addiction to a way of life that has destroyed our respect for the land, robbed our children of childhoods in open spaces, deprived them of the life lessons learned through doing and making and naturally being part of a community, deprived them of the freedom to substantially create from our own resources, deprived them of a sense of belonging.

Chatoyer and his people fought against being told what to do, what to think and how to behave by foreign invaders. They rebelled against forceful inculcation with an alien culture, which we have passively accepted. They fought for a freedom we have never known and shall never even contemplate, unless we stop to ask ourselves, "This phrase that enters our vocabulary every year- National Heroes Day- what does that really mean?"

March 2008

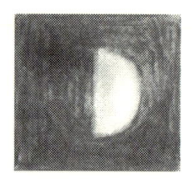

Digging to Bury Heroes

I was recently invited by the St. Vincent and the Grenadines National Trust Board to visit the archaeological dig in Argyle at the site of the International Airport construction.

I rounded up a group of college students and upon our arrival, we were greeted at the site by senior project archaeologist, Canadian Joe Moravetz. He showed us a clearing being worked on in the red clay soil, where topsoil has been removed revealing an amazing array of ancient remnants, that showed evidence of a community settlement's long house structures connected by stone pathways. It was incredibly exciting to see archaeological evidence of an organized society, dating back 2000 years, in what must be the most significant archaeological discovery in the Eastern Caribbean region.

According to Moravetz, who was in the final week of his work there, twenty human skeletons, numerous ceramic artefacts, some ninety-percent intact, have been unearthed, as well as evidence of numerous buildings. He commented that this is one of many such sites in the vicinity which, if excavated, would create a picture of how these societies lived, governed, migrated and traded throughout the region. After this initial visit, I returned with another group of fifteen student volunteers to assist the team who was running out of time to record this historical data. The educational opportunity for the youths was unsurpassed.

As the SVG National Trust makes efforts to secure and preserve what has been gleaned from the work done so far, some people may feel that local heritage is peripheral to modern development.

But evidence abounds that development based on preservation of the unique natural heritage of an island is empowering to the local communities. The preservation of cultural heritage is directly linked to a vibrant artistic culture, and stronger economies. Amerindian communities of the soil on which we live, treasured their foreparents, reflected in their practice of burying their dead in their own homes, so that the wisdom of their ancestors could assist them in their daily lives. They believed that the ground formed from the dust and blood of their ancestors was sacred ground. They understood the importance of the past in their present day lives. We have much to learn from ancient peoples' reverence for nature, revealed in their artefacts through a heightened aesthetic awareness that surpasses anything our society produces. Yet today their remnants may not be regarded as treasures to strengthen our contemporary culture but debris discarded by a culture of profit with no secure foundation.

This recent discovery could provide a valuable opportunity to build a centre for First Peoples' culture in the Organization of Eastern Caribbean States (OECS) region. It could generate visitor attraction and an important reference for connection of our young people with their own island heritage, which could effectively compensate in part, their physical and mental abandonment of their homeland.

Every March 14th, we celebrate National Heroes Day, and we are now unearthing important artefacts that could bring the national heritage alive, in a momentous discovery and contribution to our cultural heritage. Roydon Lampkin, Cultural Officer of the SVG National Trust, will be left to continue the excavation after the Canadian team leaves. He remarked that in four weeks, over two hundred groups of tourists had visited the site, demonstrating its potential to educate and attract visitors, students, international and local volunteers in the digging process. We must involve as many young people as possible in the experience, a fact that many teachers recognize, judging by the large numbers of students that have been visiting. Every Vincentian schoolchild should be

The Nature of Belonging

taken to see this site that will undoubtedly bring history alive as a subject.

If we do not act to preserve our heritage, before too long we will find that such landmarks have disappeared beneath impervious layers of concrete and tarmac, constituting a permanent burial of an honourable history based on practical wisdom. This archaeological discovery should be promoted as the major the heritage destination of the Eastern Caribbean territory. As these sites will be lost to the airport development eventually, the airport design should incorporate a large installation of the findings and site model, to educate future generations.

As long as the excavation continues locals and visitors and every returning Vincentian should be encouraged to visit it, and learn valuable aspects of our history firsthand. College students found that assisting in the dig has been an unforgettable experience, one that has made them proud to be Vincentians, one that they will pass on to future generations who may not have the extraordinary opportunity to witness the unearthing of the largest archaeological find in the Eastern Caribbean.

5th March 2009

The Most Precious Possession

One Saturday evening in April at the official residence of the Prime Minister of St. Vincent and the Grenadines, a highly unusual event took place. At the invitation of Mrs. Eloise Gonsalves, wife of the Prime Minister, a gathering of women of all ages took place to honour three distinguished women- two wives of late Governor Generals and one of a late Prime Minister. These women, Lady Antrobus, Lady Jack and Mrs Lucy-Ann Cato, are extraordinary women of their generation and that evening were surrounded by many others such as Norma Keizer, Irma Norris, Rita Nanton, and Verina Hamlet.

Dance performance and poetry reading themes acclaimed the beauty and strength of the feminine. It was an experience that impacted on everyone in unexpected ways, for these women were not only being recognized by virtue of being *wives* of men who had outstanding accomplishments. What we were really celebrating was the strength that women cultivate within themselves to survive lives filled with sacrifice. The gathering constituted a celebration of women's strength.

Many people think that the life of a woman thrust into public life is one of luxury and comfort. That may be true on the surface, but their time is not their own. The critical public eye is always upon them, they cannot always voice their own opinions and, whatever their previous vocational experience, they have to manage staff in a household that is not their family home, organize events that come with public office, and become patrons for needy causes. Whilst most people would refuse to do such a

The Nature of Belonging

job without a salary, these wives of men in public office have no personal financial reward and little public or private recognition of their efforts. It is a thankless task to which they dedicate a large portion of their lives. They also play a crucial role in their husbands' achievements by raising the children and being advisors, and giving emotional support in a relationship where their own emotional needs may remain unmet as his ambitions become fulfilled. It is a lonely and difficult path requiring boundless strength and unconditional love.

I found it wonderfully significant, yet at the same time, disconcerting, that these amazing women were being recognized that evening, only by other women. It was wonderful, because in the absence of men (except for one news reporter, who disclosed to me that he felt very uneasy among so many women!) the atmosphere resonated with beautiful feminine qualities -tremendous peace and love, creativity and grace. It is unusual in our island for women to congregate in solidarity, so caught up are they in fulfilling roles that men have prescribed for them. Many women bear their burdens in loneliness and isolation, and need more encouragement and support from eachother. But the absence of men from the gathering was at the same time disconcerting, because we need them also to uphold the strength and importance of women's role in society.

In every sphere of social, religious, political and public small island life, it seems that men of an older generation dominate, and in dominating, define women's role within constraints that are not conducive to their empowerment. Some women do not question this role-play, reinforcing denial of their own strength in the quest to gain the approval of men. A woman who circumvents the dictates of men must summon enormous strength and tread a lonely path. In thinking for herself she runs the risk of being labelled by both men and women as troublesome, aggressive and too independent. The fear of this criticism keeps many women frustrated and unfulfilled.

Birthing Moon

The younger generation do not automatically accept the dictates of the older generation, and many young women are clearing a different path from the one their mothers and grandmothers trod. They are more assertive, more expressive and more confident in charting a course navigated by their belief they can contribute in meaningful ways to their society. Though the path they are taking is not an easy one, a higher proportion of our young women are becoming fulfilled through passionate commitment to attending to their own convictions. Their male counterparts cannot dominate or influence them simply by the 'virtue' of being a man.

An older generation of Caribbean men have enjoyed a sense of omnipotence and caused women much suffering in the process. They are more likely to judge women solely in terms of their outer appearance and are tragically immune to the inner beauty that grows within a woman as she matures. As these men obsessively crave the attention of young admirers, they compromise their own maturity and opportunity for growth.

The women we paid tribute to that afternoon lived in the shadow of their husbands' careers, and in spite of, or because of this, lived lives of rich experience. They suffered in silence the loss of their own ambitions, and subsequent passing of husbands and sometimes children. Yet they are proof that suffering gives way to beauty and compassion.

The Irish poet, philosopher and Christian theologian, John O'Donohue wrote: " only the faces of those who have suffered are really beautiful. The light that suffering leaves when it goes is a very precious light." That beautiful light radiates in the faces of these ladies, and I thought how sad that our society does not recognize and treasure it. How caught up we are in commercial beauty that we fail to see the true worth of women. While many men are power driven and caught up with their outer image, sex appeal and professional accomplishments, it is woman who nurtures the spiritual strength of the inner world, born of suffering and sacrifice.

It was in tribute to these universal qualities of womanhood that this event radiated compassion that embraced everyone, old and young. Instigated by an inspired and creative Eloise Gonsalves, it was a strengthening experience, and one wonders had the men been there, would they have appreciated its true significance? For they would have had to shed their preconceptions about women, place them in the forefront and uphold their true beauty and worth.

We know from studying revolutionary movements throughout history, that instigators of change must come from within the oppressed group and as such women must act to liberate themselves from domination, through collaboration with our men, brothers and sons, a minority of whom consciously support this change. Some men are making important comments and contributions as organizers and media reporters at events for women. I salute this minority of men as our allies in combating gender inequality. They are role models for other men who have yet to question the injustices done to women. They join with us to erase centuries of exploitive conditioning that manifests in our everyday culture, to liberate us all as we move forward together building on the spirit generated by events honouring women.

Lady Gloria Antrobus in her remarks that evening, quoted poet Josiah G. Holland who wrote, " The most precious possession that ever comes to a man in this world is a woman's heart." The quote struck a chord within her audience who applauded loudly. I would venture further to say that the most precious possession a nation could ever have is the love, compassion and unbridled contribution of its women.

April 2005

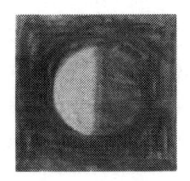

A Woman's Years – Celebrating International Women's Day 2009

I was approached for this occasion to speak about 'women and art', which, depending on one's definition of art, could be a vast or limited topic. Art, if it is viewed as painting, drawing and so on could be quite specialized as it relates to women in the Caribbean. We could sum that up as a few women artists creating some wonderful work, but not necessarily impacting on women issues generally, although some young female Vincentians are making significant inroads in this area. The limited view that we have in St Vincent of art is of course, 'commercial art', an area that is occupied by Caribbean men and expatriate women living in Caribbean islands. I don't feel exploring this area is particularly relevant to us as Caribbean women, except in that it reinforces colonial and patriarchal influences on artistic style and opportunity that dominate the commercial arts and business.

However, if we expand our definition of art to mean 'the putting together of existing things to create something new'- which all great art is- then art encompasses many more fields and activities than merely the reproduction of commercial images. It then encompasses something we do all the time and something women are particularly good at -this putting together of things to solve problems, of balancing many variables, of connective thinking, of creating relationships. So great art is essentially that- the putting together of things in a new way to solve a problem or need, that need could be functional, emotional or spiritual.

The Nature of Belonging

And this involves creative thinking and acting. And that ability is something that we women are particularly good at: mental flexibility. The shaft of nerves on our brains called the Corpus Callosum is actually thicker in women- it governs areas to do with multi-tasking and connective thinking- and actually gives us an advantage!

Many of us are conditioned to think we are not creative because we cant draw, (actually drawing is a skill that can be acquired through studied observation) but creativity is not just technical duplication, but how we utilize what we have around us to solve a problem or a need, something that has meaning, some solution to any challenge that has positive outcomes: this essentially is creativity.

So first, in my view, we have to expand our definition of what art is. There are artists who are not creative in that they may be merely copying, or reproducing what they have already done, or what someone else has done, and there are people who do not realize that they are artists who are constantly creating original solutions in the classroom, in the home, in the garden, in the workplace. So then, what is an artist if we all have this capability? Well, an artist is simply someone who has consciously chosen to develop their creative capability in productive ways. Someone who decides to create and become more adept at it – this could be in any area of the arts, or the many design fields, or in education, providing outlets for creativity in others. I know some farmers who I would call artists, who observe and react and produce in accordance with those observations.

So then 'artists' are simply the ones who facilitate making visible the invisible- through whatever medium: the creation of something original. It follows then that artists are independent thinkers, using information based on their own research and observation, though they may utilize that in partnership with others. If artists are these independent thinkers who create original solutions, it seems everyone should have an interest in creativity. I have heard it expressed that there are many great artists who are men, but very few women because women are the conveyors of culture and men express it. I would challenge this notion because women are constantly engaging in creative activity, cooking is creative, we do this all the time and yet somehow all the great chefs are men!

Women throughout history have been constantly creating useful things- environments in which relationships can flourish, be those relationships between people, through work, orienting and directing children. We are not just the conduits of culture- we act, we do and we are productive. So it's easy to see here how women as creative beings, are indispensable to functioning communities.

Artists, the ones who have chosen to develop their creative powers, are unfortunately marginalized in our society by some slight of colonial prejudice that lingers well beyond the time that its implementers have departed our shores. Artists are seen to be 'crazy', rather than considered independent thinkers. There is a prejudice against them. Women artists have a particularly hard time, as male artists far more respected than female ones, in accordance with the sexist view that independent men are admired, independent women are troublesome or freakish.

I recall last October a group of college art students, eight girls and eight boys, and I were discussing the general view of creativity in our society. I asked how many of them had been called 'weird' and all of the girls put up their hands, whereas none of the boys did, clearly indicating that with regards original thinking and expression we have different standards for boys and girls. Now, how can we harness the creativity of our women if our girls are labelled as 'weird' for thinking outside the set parameters?

To bring the implications of this into a social context: there is a lot of discussion nowadays in the Caribbean Community about 'Artists and Community transformation' and many eminent artists were the focus of the symposia at CARIFESTA X last year in Guyana. There is a document that CARICOM[11] governments are currently digesting, "Cultural Industries in CARICOM; Trade

The Nature of Belonging

and Development Challenges" about the 'creative industries' paving the way for the arts to be the centre of future economic development, not just through obvious linkages with tourism, but also in business.

But how this 'industry' is to develop without the development of creativity in our youngsters? Unless we address the capacity of our children to think and act creatively, how are we to produce great art?

And Art *is* production- it's the outcome of the creative force that we all have, consciously directed through media materials. Art as production may not transform the society, but creativity can, and the production of art and design can be a catalyst and measure of not only the transformation process but the consciousness of the people.

Now how does this relate to us as women? Women are the creators; we have the basic and inherit capacity to create life, to engender life, and this is not just a physical capability– it transmutes powerfully into our thoughts and spirits, it connects us to others, it is the source of our ability to empathize, to be compassionate and act for the greater good. Mahatma Ghandi expressed his view in his autobiography that women are spiritually advanced compared to men because they undergo the practice and discipline of sacrifice in childrearing and taking care of others. Ghandi enforced all kinds of sacrifice on himself that he recognized his wife underwent simply by virtue of being a woman.

Women have, throughout time, solved problems and challenges of survival through action, not talk. And this may be why our efforts are less recognized than those of men; we do not promote ourselves, as we are busily getting on with the next challenge!

I would also include motherhood as artistic practice, as the outcome of co-creative partnership just as gardening is the result of a co-creative relationship with nature- the creator (or artist), their medium (materials)- within an environmental context. An artist's medium could be instrumental sound, as in music, or the voice; bodily movement; paint; collage; plants and vegetables for gardeners; people in the case of a manager. Students are the medium of the creative educator, the population and other national resources those of a creative politician. Where creativity is working we see the transformation of these media into something that is for the greater good. Women can easily grasp the practical aspect of this process and as such are great implementers and contributors to society. I believe that creative and pro-active women hold the key to social transformation.

There is another aspect of great art and creativity that we as women possess readily, and that is the power of the imagination. Empathy, imagination and creativity are inextricably linked with our physical capability to gestate life. In order to achieve some of the things we do, we have to be able to imagine them possible first. To facilitate our reconnection with the power of possibility is creativity in action.

So the topic of my discourse has become not about women artists but about all women as creators- as the creative beings that we are. Many aspects of our culture are disrespectful towards women at all levels of society. The culture of domination and suppression focuses on materialism rather than on the value of life, creativity and living systems. This is the cultural framework within which women have accepted belittlement and reduced to fulfil the wishes of men rather than live their true creative power and potential.

Returning to the original theme of 'Women and Art', when I first contemplated this topic I thought separately about what it means to be a Caribbean woman and what it means to be an artist. I realized then that to be both is indeed an extraordinary and unique experience and one that is not understood nor accounted for in our male dominated society that has a conformist view of women and also shuns creative thinking. Caribbean women artists endure immense struggle through racism, overt sexism and the crippling prejudice towards the creative arts. A woman artist

The Nature of Belonging

of colour, therefore, has to be exceptionally strong on the receiving end of a triply compounded prejudice.

This is a predicament that few people, understandably, are willing to endure. Hence many women never express their creative and independent thoughts and ideas. But to survive as a Caribbean woman artist is to discover that one's creativity becomes the path through which new and meaningful realities are sought. Creative action and nurturing creativity in others, liberate us from the bondage of racism and sexism. Creative expression provides the experience of what it means to be free. It gives us strength and empowerment, a glimpse of indigenous life in the past and of future possibilities. The negative projections from society vanish as we create a new reality for ourselves and for our children.

As I live this struggle on a daily basis, the concern becomes how to share the sense of liberation with others suppressed by the conditioning that to be black or mixed race is to be inferior, that to be a woman is to subordinate, and to be an artist is to be stupid and useless to society. To be proud of our culture is to acknowledge our exceptional ancestral genetics; to be a woman is to know pain and the power of compassion and to recognize that we cannot have one without the other. To be an artist is to find the true cultural sovereignty and divinity in Nature.

The Caribbean Woman Artist then, is the bearer of a precious legacy of survival, empowerment and community. And whilst there are few historically acclaimed women artists and almost no well-known Caribbean women artists, I know some young Vincentians who it has been my privilege to guide on their creative journeys and I'd like to say a few words about them:

The most suppressed person in society must be the poor, black, young, female who chooses to become an artist. Such are some of the young women that I have worked with and learned from as they express their experience as young women in a troubled society. Their art has enabled them to articulate the pain and frustration of emotional and sexual abuse, their innermost feelings about attaining womanhood, their questioning and challenging patriarchal religious indoctrination, their love of nature, their depression, addictions, and suicidal intentions. Their art expresses all of this, these young women are in our communities articulating our collective suffering in truthful picture of what it means to be black, female and creative. Some of them are studying abroad now achieving awards in Cuba, US and Canada.

Their work speaks of enormous creative insights, of the ancestral legacy, of pride, identity and courage. They tell the story of Caribbean people, and like their enslaved ancestors, these girls have endured abuse that has made them desperately unhappy, they have turned to their creative powers to overcome the negativity and be healed. They have expressed their pain in their work and risen above it to become strong, confident and truthful in their knowledge of themselves. And now they smile and laugh a lot. They are fun to be with. Some are teaching and inspiring other youngsters.

This is the transformational power of creativity that can heal our youth and our communities. From these young hearts and minds, the articulation of suffering of women everywhere is made visible through images, audible through poetry. They provide therapy for generations of Caribbean women whose memories resonate in contemporary images, within new voices that enable us to move on, released from prejudice and painful projection. To move on into a space where we are proud of a heritage that found beauty in being a woman. The new voices exemplify the strength and dignity of our ancestors watching over them with pride and love, ever to guide them to fulfil what they have come into this life to do.

As women, every day our beauty is wrenched from us through the expectation of surrender and subordination; of who we should be and how we should behave. The struggle is a silent one for all but the strongest; among them our women artists strengthened by their creative journeys. They have held tight to their own ideas and expression. They have retained the truthful link to their ancestry and heritage. Art is their transformation and liberation.

The Nature of Belonging

The young women I have worked with can ably guide others through personal transformation. They could be leaders within the society but will they be allowed to lead? Will we overcome the compounded prejudice towards our women artists to let the ancestral light illuminate and emancipate the minds and hearts of all of our women?

Caribbean poet Grace Nichols has beautifully captured our collective journey in her epilogue, "I Is a long-Memoried Woman":

I have crossed an ocean I have lost my tongue
From the root of the old one
A new one has sprung.

Unforgiving as the course of justice
Irreversible as my scars and fate
I am here
A woman …….with all my lives Strung out like beads before me

It isn't privilege or pity that I seek
It isn't reverence or safety
Quick happiness or purity
    But
The power to be what I am/ a woman
Charting my own future/ a woman
Holding my beads in my hand.

(Speech given to celebrate International Women's Day, The Prime Minister's Residence, Kingstown, March 20th 2009)

Message from the Birthing Moon

As surely as the moon revolves around the earth, babies are born to depart as elders. What will be their contribution? How can we ensure that they live a good life with their gifts intact?

Through welcoming them saying:
>"We are happy you are here.
>We need your gifts.
>We are yours and you are free."

4.

Earth Moon

April

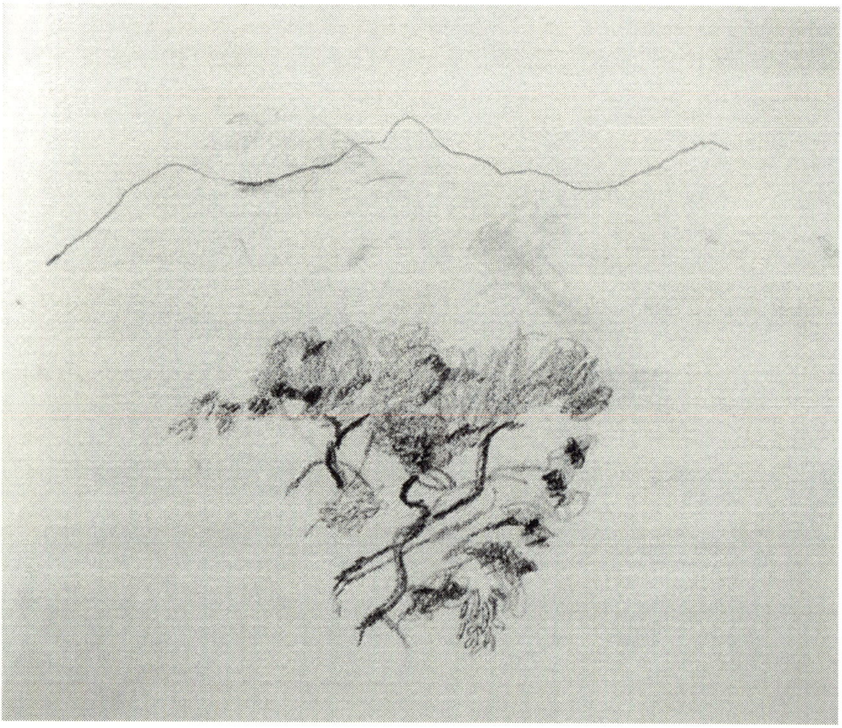

I live and breathe the mountain. Peacefully I reconcile my days into Belonging

The Greatest of Wastes

In 1929 Russell Smith, himself an American, wrote, "Without any doubt, the American is the most destructive animal that ever trod the earth."[12] Smith was referring to how American settlers were destroying the land through farming methods that cause soil erosion. He noticed that the methods of farming they used had been brought from Europe where the land type and climate is different from that of the American continent, of which the Caribbean is geographically part.

The white settlers of America brought farming methods that were developed for flat land in Europe and when used on the mountains in the Americas, land devastation through erosion was the result. The methods involved tilling and loosening the soil for planting which was then washed away in heavy rains. This system was developed in a climate of light drizzle and cooler temperatures, but the effect in tropical mountainous terrain was destructive. Instead of developing more suitable practices for mountainous areas with heavy rainfall, the settlers moved onto another areas, repeating the malpractice until all the fertile land had been eroded. In the American cotton belt where plantations were established, some countries were reported one-third worn out before 1850.

In his book, 'Tree Crops: A Permanent Agriculture', Russell Smith wrote:

"In this way we have already destroyed the homelands fit for the sustenance of millions. We need an enlarged definition for treason. Some people should not be allowed to sing "My Country." They are destroying it too rapidly."

Meanwhile, on the plantations in Caribbean islands, agricultural workers had been inculcated by Europeans to use the same destructive farming methods, which are in use to this present day. In our own islands we can see how this same pattern of land erosion is proceeding rapidly. We may comfort ourselves with the thought that we are blessed with rich fertile soil, revealing ignorance of how once the trees are cut and the land loosened with the hoe, the heavy rains will wash away the topsoil. Invariably this soil, rich in nutrients, is only a couple of feet deep, yet it has taken thousands of years to form.

Russell Smith refers to the destructive sequence of forest, field, plough, desert. In our small islands it is forest, field, hoe, desert.

Smith identified field wash, or soil erosion, in the United States, Latin America, Africa, and many other parts of the world, as the greatest and most menacing of all resource wastes. He said that:

> "It removes the basis of civilization and of life itself. It is far worse than burning a city. A burned city can be rebuilt. A field that is washed away is gone for ages. Hence the Old World saying, 'After the man the desert.' "

To demonstrate repairing the damage done, Smith, pioneered a farming system he called 'mountain agriculture' in which small landowners would manage, devotedly and skilfully, a diversified, locally-adapted system of tree crops, pastures, animals, and row crops. This mixed farming system is based on the principles of agro-forestry, a natural farming system that uses nature's patterns as its basis and that ensures building back the soil for future generations. Indigenous people used this type of cultivation. Estate workers practiced mixed farming on their own small plots, from which they supplied all their own food needs. This practice became less common when farmers were encouraged to grow for

The Nature of Belonging

export, but it can be re-established in our own gardens, no matter how small, and on larger scales is critical to future food security. By mixing fruit and forest trees with tropical root crops, peas and vines such as passion fruit and beans, the land can be saved and forests regenerated.

Those of us who understand what this means should never see the landscape in the same way again. We should feel that we have acquired deeper understanding of the soil, which is our heritage and legacy. We are connected to it and it to us. However much commercial culture has conditioned us to believe otherwise, the land and its soil is our future. With this realization comes the responsibility to play whatever part we can in its regeneration, through promoting and practicing mountain agriculture.

Russell Smith dedicated his writing "to persons of imagination who love trees and love their country," and his practical philosophy is even more applicable now as when he wrote it eighty years ago. He pleads with his fellow countrymen and women for "a new patriotism," expressing amazement at "patriots" who are willing to fight and perhaps die to defend from foreign threat a country that they themselves are destroying.

He would be horrified now to learn that some governments, not satisfied with destroying their own countries, proceed to plunder others for their resources and have extended the destruction to human life as well as that of the soil.

Meanwhile, following in the footsteps of the Americans, we seem to be competing for the position of the "most destructive animal that ever trod the earth", for as we clear more and more forest, till more soil, build bigger houses and watch without concern as our topsoil washes away, we are surely the most destructive animal that ever trod these islands.

September 2007

Earth Moon

Human Beings – an Endangered Species?

The creative force of a landscape that captivated my imagination during my first visit to St. Vincent was tangible through its changing moods, its dramatic views and its unspoiled slopes. After living in the rigid confines of suburban Port-of-Spain and having to travel far from the city to breathe nature's energy, St. Vincent was by comparison a Gift of Nature. But even then, I was not aware exactly how precious our landscape is.

During a trip to Mexico in late 2003 to learn about natural building techniques on a reforestation project[13], I was describing the farmland where I live, work, and create, to a group of Mexican farmers. I listed all the trees and resources in our vicinity that can be utilized in natural building - things that we in St. Vincent take for granted like bamboo, clay soil, banana fibre, teak and mahogany, razor grass, aside from the foodstuffs, fruits and vegetables. As I spoke I saw mouths dropping open on the faces all around me, 'But you live in Paradise!' the workshop leader, Alejandra, exclaimed. I was amazed to learn in Mexico that the eroded landscape, where at best the growing season is only four months per year, was once lush forest. In the last few centuries, forests had been cut down for building and planting crops, and the land became a soil-eroded desert. Because there are no longer trees growing on it, the topsoil has washed away and the rest of the earth has dried out. The earth became so compacted that it turned into the desert terrain we now associate with Mexico. Along with the disappearance of the trees went all the birds and animals. The Mexicans now struggle to survive off this land, which is so hard

The Nature of Belonging

that they can cut blocks out of the ground to build houses. My friends there are working hard to reforest large areas. No wonder they referred to my description of St. Vincent as 'paradise'.

This experience was an unforgettable lesson for me in the devastating effects of deforestation on a huge country. Upon doing more research I discovered that practically every continent in the world has been ravaged by deforestation – starting five thousand years ago in the lush valley of Mesopotamia by the Euphrates River, which is now a barren desert and occupied by part of Irac. The Sahara desert similarly was once covered in the Sahara forest. Continents throughout the world have suffered a similar fate through deforestation to build and fuel the growth of modern civilizations. The effects on landscapes and their people have been dramatic. It is not surprising that many of the Caribbean islands have been affected similarly. Topography that appears to be 'natural' is in fact the secondary or tertiary attempt of nature to recuperate from exhaustive land clearance for plantations during the colonial period. Our neighbours Antigua and Anguilla, and Barbados have little remaining forest and consequently no rivers. Grenada and St. Lucia have only a fraction of their original forest and diminished rainfall as a result. The most mountainous islands of the Caribbean, Dominica and St. Vincent have kept proportionally more of their indigenous forest, due to the inaccessibility of the topography for cultivation.

After directly observing the results of conversion of densely forested areas into an eroded desert landscape, I now realize precisely how precious a resource we have in our rainforest; how its life sustaining nature literally holds the earth together, providing a habitat for many species of animals, flora and fauna. It is the reason we have adequate rainfall providing our clear, safe drinking water, which has become an expensive commodity in countries that have undergone extensive deforestation. It's also the reason why we have potentially lush soil for cultivation.

Against the global backdrop of deforestation, we become more aware of the precious resource we have in our rainforest and the need to protect what is left. Now, at less than 30 percent of its original area, it is decreasing by more than 1 percent each year as farmers illegally cut away the edges of the protected rainforest to clear land for planting. The effects are devastating on the environment. According to the Worldwatch Institute in 1990 alone the earth's surface lost over 480 billion tons of valuable topsoil. Our soil is washed into rivers and oceans as a result of the extensive use of chemical fertilizers, deforestation and poor farming practices.

Yet it is still common practice in St. Vincent to clear large areas, not only for agriculture but also for building houses. Trees that have taken many years to grow are cut down at random, despite the valuable work they are doing. The environmental movement in St. Vincent and the Grenadines has yet to gather strength, but it is time to become more aware of the destruction of the delicately balanced ecosystems that starts with tree cutting.

John Roulac places the issue of deforestation more clearly into a global context:

> "If our current cycle of deforestation and drought continues unchecked, many biologists and scientists believe that much of the world's remaining forests and productive lands will disappear in the early part of the 21st century. With the soil will go the earth's plants, animals and perhaps human beings. Losing our productive lands may cause humans to be considered an endangered species"[14]

There are many things we can do within our own lives, homes and communities to address the situation. First, we need to become more informed about environmental degradation resulting from our intervention in natural processes. We can start by observing our own surroundings and educating our children to play a critical role in the future protection of the environment. Cultivation of higher quality vegetables for local and niche export markets will reduce the use of chemical fertilizers which can be replaced by vegetable waste, animal dung, green fertilizers (plants, grasses, fast growing trees and legume vines) and waste paper to create compost. We can also plant trees and shrubs in many places- community groups can work together on this, as they have done in Villa to beautify the roadside to Villa beach.

We are extremely fortunate that St. Vincent's mountainous landscape has been saved the scale of environmental destruction that has drastically affected other small islands, although much of our landscape has already become degraded. Unfortunately our island's partial preservation is not an outcome of human intervention and in no way reflects heightened environmental awareness of her citizens. Had her topography been more easily accessible to the plough, no doubt she would have suffered a similar fate. Nature built protective measures into her own physique. But now she needs our cooperation through concerted efforts to save what is mercifully left.

Even if we are not nature lovers, surely the experience of eking out an existence on compacted land is something we would not consciously choose; something that for millions of others around the globe, like my Mexican friends, is no longer an option, as it is for us living obliviously in 'paradise'.

December 2003

Coastal Desert

From the vantage point of Fort Charlotte there is a sight that should shock all Vincentians- expanses of exposed earth that each year moves further inland with each dry season. All trees have gone, vegetation expired, the earth is hard, and even animals can't graze on it. The land is barren. If the present rate of environmental degradation is allowed to continue through land clearing, coastal degradation will move inland like the once well-watered forested islands of Anguilla, Antigua or Canouan, where productive cultivation is minimal and potable water is imported or produced by expensive desalination plants.

As a nation we are shockingly complacent about the rate at which we are losing our fertile lands. Since Independence, consecutive governments have been significant perpetrators of environmental degradation in three ways. Firstly, by failing to control rampant clearing of the land for monocrop cultivation and residential development. This type of clearing which eradicates all trees and natural habitats has a domino effect on the whole island's ecology. Secondly, governments have not seriously investigated the benefits of renewable energy sources like solar and wind power, but have embarked on fossil fuel intensive projects e.g. diesel-generated power plants. They have also promoted farming practices that degrade and will eventually exhaust the soil. Thirdly, there has been minimal public education in recent decades pertaining to the importance of maintaining the natural environment, which can be done largely through cultural awareness programmes in schools.

Promoting environmental awareness seems to have been contrary to the aims of certain government development projects, that have been profit-driven with short-term interests rather than providing sustainably for the future generations. In recent decades successive governments have been updated through the work of dedicated individuals in the Forestry division in the Ministry of Agriculture who have collected information on land degradation, encroachment on the rainforest, and the decline in river water levels. But still the destruction continues without institutional will to act to the contrary.

In this way, through a combination of action and neglecting to act, all governments have been the main perpetrators of environmental destruction since Independence. In 1980 we had forty-five percent of original rainforest which is now less than thirty percent and is declining every day, but few people seems aware of its implications island wide.

Private individuals take their cue from government in the uncontrolled cutting of valuable trees to clear land for building and replacing it with lawn and concrete. I recently witnessed the cutting of a huge mango tree in a residential area that was bordering some land being cleared for construction on the windward side of St.Vincent. The tree was not obstructing the planned development and would have provided shade, retained water in the soil with its roots, produced delicious fruit and a habitat for birds and insects in an otherwise built-up area. But what compounds the tragedy is that the development is for tourist apartments. Common sense tells us that many tourists come here from urban areas in the industrialized north to experience tropical nature, so why are we destroying the very things that attract them? The Mustique Company exert strict control on the cutting of trees in Mustique Island, but on mainland St. Vincent, our precious green neighbourhoods have no protection.

We need not wait any longer to put a halt to the systematic destruction of the earth that could provide more than enough food, shelter and water for the whole of St. Vincent and the

Grenadines. In the same way that cutting down trees is destroying the environment, planting trees is the single most important action in saving it. We may wait a long time for governments to accept the need for a reforestation program, as their projects seem to entail large-scale deforestation. The private sector, communities and individuals must begin to save the environment. There is an abundance of information available through the Internet on environmental issues, and we can start in our own yards by planting fruit trees, and creating kitchen gardens. Any tree planted and protected will assist in bringing the earth to life and creating shade and rainfall. Each person and family can play their part in regenerating the soil around their homes and communities.

In global environmental initiatives women, youth and the civil society are performing key roles in promoting sustainable development in small islands. Collectively, the efforts of its citizens can help to bring back the natural beauty that St. Vincent and the Grenadines is renowned for and that is fast disappearing from the coast inland, nowhere more obvious than from Fort Charlotte.

It is an interesting historical fact that when the Fort was constructed by the British, its canons turned inland on the Garifuna who fought for two centuries to protect their beloved island from foreign invaders. Let us hope our visitors when they go there, keep looking out to sea and don't turn their heads inland. For one glimpse of the coastal desert we are creating will horrify the environmentally conscious and create the correct impression that the island's inhabitants are its own worst enemies.

March 2005

The Nature of Belonging

Earth Day Remembrance

Earth Day comes and goes in our calendar but what lasting effect does it leave?

In a rousing Earth Day speech in Iowa, President Obama declared a "New Era for Energy" as he rallied the population of the United States in a joint mission to tackle what he referred to as the "energy crisis and global economic crisis." He outlined practical things that individuals can do to save energy in their households, such as changing light bulbs to energy-saving ones; and the importance of everyone joining in the effort towards a common goal. Whilst he focused on household economies and ways to make sensible savings, he was generally appealing to Americans to change their lifestyle based on excessive consumption.

I first visited the US in 2003 when I went to study natural building in Athens County, Ohio. Having gleaned some initial impressions of the American people from those I met whilst travelling in other countries, I was surprised to meet, on American soil, a group of atypical characters from various backgrounds (they referred to themselves as 'outsiders') united in their intention to tackle environmental issues through recycling, green architecture, permaculture design, and renewable energy technology. Several years later these 'outsiders' were gratified to hear their new President recommending their lifestyle choices to the whole nation!

Environmentalism became a recognized movement in the U.S. in the 1950s and 60s- when leading environmentalists, such as Rachel Carson, advocated a healthy chemical-free lifestyle based on the land, eating what can be grown locally to support local farmers and local community economies. The natural building movement that followed has been steadily growing since 1990, and has spawned a revival of green (ecological) architecture designed to have low impact on the environment, through appropriate selection of materials and building processes. Where groups of environmentally conscious people came together, they established eco-villages, or 'intentional communities' that have emerged into a worldwide movement, through the Global Ecovillage network and the Ecovillage Network of the Americas. These settlements are living examples of participatory organization and innovative problem solving, through designing renewable energy systems, organic gardens, schools' and school curricula, outreach programmes and holistic health centres.

The basic priority practice of such communities is environmental conservation, through land regeneration, sustainable land use and community self-reliance. Intentional communities appeal to those who aspire to a fuller life of community belonging.

President Obama appealed for the majority of the population to take on a similar consciousness, ridding themselves of the notion that being American means being individualistic and consuming excessively, to embracing a proactive attitude in implementing solutions through making lifestyle changes. He disclosed his plan to create millions of jobs in an alternative energy industry.

Here in St Vincent and the Grenadines, the natural environment is seen as important primarily to attract tourists. But there are many reasons why it must be protected for the local population, not simply as a picturesque backdrop, but for research into how it functions optimally, providing resources for survival and sustainable development. Accessible sources of energy from wind, sun, and sea are yet to be harnessed. Deforestation should be halted with immediate effect because forests provide oxygen, ample rainfall, ground cooling, prevent soil erosion and promote biodiversity, all of which are essential to sustainable development.

This is the larger picture, that once seen clearly, should arrest our negligence towards environmental degradation and divert us from wanton tree cutting, polluting with synthetic chemicals, burning fires

The Nature of Belonging

and burying non-biodegradable waste, towards addressing how our communities can replenish for future generations that which has been removed. Though we may agree with such a noble ideal intellectually, we can see that a movement does not begin without concerted action, and progress does not occur without *sustained* concerted action. It's easy to sound like an environmentalist without having environmental consciousness, like the 'social-activist' who resists meaningful change when it compromises self-interests; or a Christian in name only, but not in moral behaviour. Our effectiveness in noble causes comes about through doing something practical. Deanne Soares, a Jamaican gardener/poet reflected on this in an online journal:

> "We Christians get very animated at best when matters of sexual license are being discussed, but generally do not demonstrate any similar passion when matters related to our stewardship of the environment are raised. I cannot ever remember hearing a sermon in church berating anyone for wasting electricity or polluting the environment. Actually I was once ridiculed for suggesting that the lights be switched off if the sun was shining. I know of no festival in the Christian calendar that is a call to plant trees, despite sharing the same scriptural edicts that have prompted our Jewish brothers and sisters. We also harshly criticize so called pagan and primitive religions that saw their deities in the natural world and as a result treated the natural world with awe and respect. There is no excuse for indifference by Christians, to matters of an environmental nature. Individual as well as corporate entities must begin to feel responsible for implementing the necessary changes."[15]

Deanne expresses her conviction that to address urgent environmental challenges, words must be put into action. World leaders are currently being implored by their people to commit to a strong climate change agreement. President Obama, along with other leaders around the world, is not initiating action, but responding to the call for action of the environmental movement to address national issues within the context of global climate change. World leaders are listening and responding to citizens who as relentless 'outsiders' paving the way, dared to adopt more conscious lifestyles. As wo/mankind shifts consciousness, through force of necessity, from the individualism of the Industrial Age towards the inclusivism of the Environmental Age, the practical ideals of those outsiders, are to become daily life realities for everyone. Their movement has gained increasing momentum through people-powered networking through the Internet, which President Obama utilized to maximum effect in his presidential campaign.

The global environmental movement is thus poised to reach a critical mass. Caribbean island fragile island ecosystems are particularly vulnerable to the effects of climate change, and we cannot languish in resistance to the global momentum. We need everyone- religious groups, the youth, the elderly, teachers, students, government departments- to work together to make our contribution to the local, regional and global effort. Governments everywhere can galvanize the masses effectively through incorporating environmental education into school curricula; promoting sustainable agricultural practices; creating incentives for environmentally sound business practices and eco-commerce; commitment to sustainable tourism initiatives that stimulate cultural and environmental conservation.

In 2001 I was invited by the Caribbean Conservation Association to Trinidad to collaborate with environmentalists and other artists in devising creative ways of involving communities in environmental action. Many creative projects were devised there that await implementation. Artists have a significant role to play in the environmental age, ensuring that their creative ideas stimulate the environmental consciousness of their communities. The arts have a critical role to play in raising awareness through drama, dance, music, literary arts, video and installations. Earth Day each year would be unforgettable if it were marked by a pledge by all groups and organizations to commit to environmental awareness building endorsed in practical terms through various avenues, including the arts. Every school should have its productive organic garden, every watershed its local market, every community its recycling centre and a seed exchange for kitchen gardening. These are simple initial measures that could generate more secure communities to cope with the effects of the energy crisis and the global economic crisis.

When lobbied by a group of British youngsters to attend climate change talks due to take place in Copenhagen in December 2009, British Prime Minister Gordon Browne said:

> "we can change the way the world works- the whole world must come together and say "we want the world to change for the better" and we can make it happen."

In his Agenda for Reform that he delivered at the same Climate Change Summit, he stated:

> "As global communications networks bring more and more people together, we are finding that the values they share are a greater inspiration to action than those which divide them."[16]

Leaders now depend on ordinary people who have been working together across the globe to make the most of their local resources in partnership and understanding of this critical human transition in global history. Those who view conscious alignment with the earth as a sacrificial 'making do with less', may not yet grasp that the 'more' that they have in mind is detrimental to us all, particularly nature herself. As we create alternatives out of what we didn't realize we have, the environmental age is not one of sacrifice but one that brings many benefits; not least of all the rebuilding of self-reliant communities, broken down for too long by ignorance of the true significance of Earth Day.

April/December 2009

Message from the Earth Moon

Nature's essential elements- air, space, water, sunlight, earth- make themselves visible though rivers, trees and plants, rocks, the ocean, sky wind and rain, and give us life.

Through what immortal force, will we cease to violate this fundamental truth and work in partnership with her to create an art of the highest order: a civilization in which nature can thrive as well in our presence as she could in our absence?

5.

Sea Water Moon

May

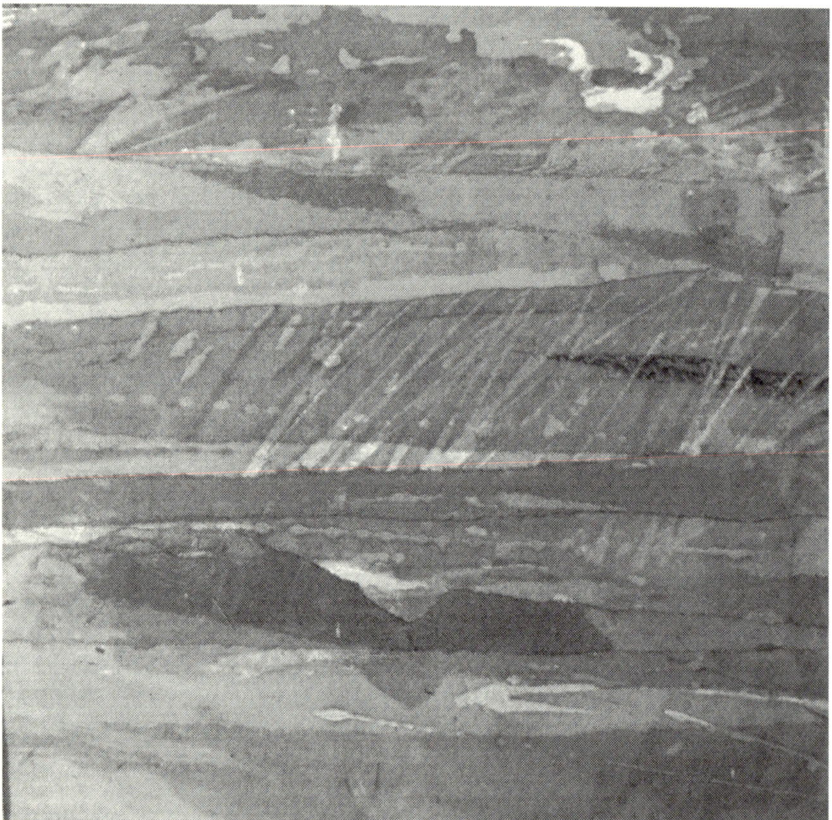

Mountain water becomes the sea. The mountain deep and steep. Undulation. Wave. Motion. Things learned.

The Nature of Belonging

Childhood Memories are made of this...........

In 1992 a few months after arriving in St Vincent I, had noticed that the typical primary schools in St Vincent and the Grenadines had very basic classrooms with no books, visual aids or children's artwork on the walls. Broken furniture and gloomy atmospheres contrasted starkly to the schools in Trinidad where I had lived before coming to St. Vincent. I was surprised to see school environments so uninspiring here. It seemed strange to me at the time, in a place where the landscape was then unrivalled in its beauty, that children should spend their school days captive in dull and uncreative rooms.

Another observation that disturbed me all those years ago was that our favourite beach nearest to town, Ottley Hall, was to become an Italian owned marina project- the community beach and old barracks would be remodelled into a marina, hotel, supermarket, and a playground for the rich. We know now that this plan never fully materialized but nevertheless, one of St. Vincent's most beautiful beaches has gone forever.

I remarked on these two observations- the condition of schools and destruction of the beach- in conversations with local people in Bequia and St Vincent. Their response was that I sounded like the 'opposition' and I must have been talking to Ralph Gonsalves. But I had no idea about politics here or who the opposition leader was. To have simply made a comment based on observation and to be labelled as 'opposition' was my introduction to the obsessive grip of party politics that rules the nation. Of course, many years later, I am not so naïve about the ferocity of party politics, nor of the reason why there is little change in the stark and uncompromising learning environments of our children.

After the local community was refused access to Ottley Hall beach in 1992, afternoons with my young children were spent on our local beach at Buccament Bay. This became as much home for them as the lush yard where we grew vegetables and tended our goats and sheep. On many evenings we would relax in the sea, play cricket on the beach, watch the sunset, admire the unspoilt view towards the rainforest, mingle with the community and on early weekend mornings help fishermen bring in the seine. We shared those experiences regularly with our valley community, people from several villages united in the cradle of mountain ridges, gleaning sustenance of mind, body and spirit at the water's edge where generations before have done the same.

We all have our stories and special experiences from nestling into the natural curve of the Bay. Just last Sunday I ventured once more to Buccament Bay with my son, now 24 years of age. He had not swum there for over a year and his anguish was visible when he saw the radical change that the beach of his childhood has undergone in the process of conversion into a high-end tourism complex. I observed his obvious discomfort through his facial expression, evidence of thoughts going through his mind- this was where ten years ago he learned to drive, where he fished and dived from the rocks. I saw, not the jubilance that he used to enjoy here, but a serious questioning and expression of having one's roots shaken and torn.

I was witnessing the experience of countless other youths from the valley villages, whose connection with their beach has been wrenched away, pushed to extremes of the water's edge as outsiders in their own land. An enclosure on the black sand beach prepares to receive thousands of tons of white sand from shores of other lands, ironically symbolic of the replacement of the local community with outsiders from a different climate and culture. Such a monumental restructuring of a nation's heritage causes psycho-spiritual damage in rural communities. It is not directly

The Nature of Belonging

quantifiable but highly discernable in the expressions of all who reminisce over happy days of heading out for the beach cook, the sap in the sea, the tri-tri......

We may have seen the last generation of Vincentian youth whose memories will be of personal connection to their landscape, particularly to that beach. Their national identity is compromised as their connection with the landscape is wrenched away by increasingly competitive developers, wrestling the natural heritage out of the hands and memories of its rightful heirs and owners. The interests of the investors take priority in the development strategy over the experiences of the local people who created a unique culture that is so easily destroyed but not easily rebuilt. A culture of experience and expression disappears under edifices of concrete and that we locals will never be welcome inside.

The Buccament valley community has been dealt a harsh and uncompromising hand- what the community created has been dismantled. Their loyalty to successive politicians and their parties has not brought success in preserving their unique culture of survival inextricably linked to the land and the sea. These are the same misgivings that I voiced so many years ago and was told that I must be 'opposition', aligned to someone I had never met. Ironically the opposition then forms the government now -how short are our memories in politics. But the living memories of a people of experiences and interactions that give them lasting connection to intangible culture, to their landscape and heritage, these are memories that cannot be erased so easily, and though they may not be articulated by those who have been suppressed for so long, these memories are real and provide indicators of what a community must protect.

Is the development we want to see, one where a young person's childhood becomes history within ten short years, where the roots of our youth are torn away from them leaving them to produce future generations spiritually impoverished, subconsciously grieving for their culture of community that they will never know?

Whilst natural heritage is destroyed, classrooms remain woefully the same. Places where our children eked out the few precious joys of childhood will now provide pleasurable memories for wealthy visitors, whilst those experiences they would rather forget-within dreaded classrooms- have been preserved for generations to come.

December 2006

The Nature of Belonging

Hungry for Poverty

'Make Poverty History' was the slogan for the global demonstrations of July 2005, raising awareness of the need for poverty eradication. A series of huge music concerts was organized worldwide to lobby the attention of the leaders of the eight leading nations in the world, at the summit on 7th July in Edinburgh, UK. The concerts and demonstrations were a shining example of how people from all over the world can come together to make their voice heard in the political arena. Many programmes about Africa were aired on BBC World, showing the various challenges facing poor Africans in their daily lives. Watching the footage one was overwhelmed by a sense of injustice, but the strength and dignity of the African people was nevertheless noticeable in some of the most desperate conditions that humanity has ever endured.

In one such programme, agricultural experts were being interviewed in a Sudanese rural community. The experts had been called in from Europe and Australia to teach the locals how to farm for export -the new methods of planting in rows, not the traditional scattering of seeds seeds, and using chemicals because in the words of the expert "the land is so depleted you cannot grow anything without chemical fertilizer." At this point tears came to my eyes because I realized that these methods the Africans are so readily taking on, will simply lead them into further dependency and their land into further degradation. As we have seen here in St. Vincent and the Grenadines, chemical fertilizers will not build up the land for the future. They further exhaust the soil and create the need for more chemicals that have to be purchased from industrialized nations.

We have also been taught an artificial method of farming that creates more dependency.

Our African sisters and brothers, were assured that their energy supply would be in the form of a foreign installed generator, not from solar panels that could sustainably capture the blazing sunlight and provide power for households and irrigation systems. The farmers were being led into further dependence by experts representing the interest of their own countries, directing them to grow crops for export instead of assisting them to feed their own families. Some African farmers realize they have a better chance of survival if they remain farming on a small scale independently for the local market, they can be more flexible and not incur the expense of inputs.

Using different farming methods, the land in Africa could be organically replenished and provide enough food for its own populations. The widespread assistance needed is to establish diverse sustainable farming systems. In their desperation, many African farmers feel they have no choice: they are lead to believe, like us, that they are being assisted, when they are really being coerced into further dependence on industrialized nations.

Much of the debt relief being granted to developing countries by the G8 (or the "greedy 8" as some people are referring to the eight most powerful countries) is relief from debt that was incurred from loans from the World Bank and IMF, representing the industrialized nations through specified structural adjustment programmes that have not benefited developing countries economies in the long-term. On the other hand, the developed countries benefit as much of this aid money is returned through consultants and contractors fees and purchase of materials and equipment.

We in the Eastern Caribbean have fallen prey to the same folly in agriculture and other areas of manufacturing. We have swallowed the pill of dependency whole and continue to let our land and culture be exploited. If this sounds extreme, consider the banana 'crisis' that descended upon us in the late 1990s, when our farmers were dictated to in terms of the shape and colour of the banana, the exact method of tagging, fertilizing, trading and packing. The process necessitated intensive inputs to be purchased from the UK. The end result was geared to the artificial visual preferences of the European consumer. More than twenty-five percent of the bananas were rejected in the field to rot, while there was a shortage of bananas in the local and regional markets. The effect of this was to cripple banana production so that only the larger farmers could survive this 'structural adjustment'. Mr Masanobu Fukuoka, who practiced natural farming for fifty years in Japan captures this process in simple terms when he says:

> " So from the time just before the fruit has been harvested to the time it is shipped out and put on the display counter, five or six chemicals are used. This is not to mention the chemical fertilizers and sprays that were used while the crops were growing in the field. And all this because the consumer wants to buy fruit just a little more attractive. This little edge of preference has put the farmer in a real predicament."[17]

Whilst the survival of our farmers and agricultural workers is literally in the hands of outside powers, can we really talk of attaining independence in the islands? Mr. Fukuoka calls modern farming "manufacturing", and the imbalance it has caused is similar to other types of industrial manufacturing, where the land is being decimated and polluted whilst power and money become the accepted goals.

Like the Caribbean territories, Africa needs farming methods that rebuild the soil, back to its original state. Before man interfered with nature's balance, forests covered Africa. The transformation from forest to desert has occurred through bad farming practices. We have not reached the point that Africa has as yet, where many people are starving. But at the current rate of modernization of farming, construction, and unsustainable development, the remaining rainforest and topsoil that has taken thousands of years for nature to develop will be cleared away within two decades and we will be left with a desert.

In weeping for the plight of our African brothers and sisters, I also quietly mourn us islanders as we arrogantly destroy the very substance of life. For many at death's door must use whatever help comes along, but we in our well-fed complacency are blind to the fact that we have choices beyond the purely profit-driven. While we pray for the millions of Africans dying unnecessarily that poverty will be history, let us hope that our unsustainable practices will not make poverty our future. Hope alone is not enough though- only conscious action today can save us from being tomorrow's hungry and impoverished.

August 2005

Tracks and Pathways

A sequence of thoughts came to me whilst watching a lizard pass across the window ledge. I wondered if he or she knew where they were going as an external fixed destination, or whether they were being lead by an innate force through each sporadic burst of movement. The territorial lizard had been patrolling its turf with regularity and I assumed s/he must be fully aware of its orientation within the larger complex of lizard reality. This observation led me to ponder similarly about people's movements and activities.

It seems to me that people focus on one of two approaches to life. One group set off knowing where they are going towards an externally sourced destination. This group would include students with set (often parental) goals and prescribed career paths of becoming a doctor, lawyer, architect, politician, businessperson etc. Their life is perceived from within the construct of their ambition, possibly structured as incremental stages in a linear, logical fashion. For the other group, despite being pressurised by society to perform otherwise, there are no prescribed goals or lofty achievement targets. They may choose (or have no choice) to live life in a completely different way. Their perception of life is not linear, but is constantly fed through an immediate connection with their surroundings, people and the environment. Their life's learning comes through this immediate experience rather than listed texts of profession.

With constant awareness of what's happening in the vicinity and the habit of constantly responding to it, this second group are prone to changing their life course based on their experiences.

These would be the artists, farmers, writers, musicians, creative thinkers.

Obviously these groups are not mutually exclusive, creative thinkers do plan and study at university; planners may be creative; with a wild stretch of the imagination we could have creative politicians: but it seems that whichever one of these two perspectives we choose to travel, creates our perception of daily life. Moreover, one path- the one along prescribed career lines - is held up as the better one and touted to students as 'doing something important for society' versus wasting your time. This is the track of academia, becoming qualified and quantifiably successful in climbing the social ladder. The other path has been associated with dropping out of society, being less intelligent, 'or not so bright', and generally less use to society. Yet, in all these assumptions, we have been gravely misguided. Upon inspection, we uncover the prescribed path of success and 'professionalism' as a common quest for individual wealth and status, and not necessarily for the betterment of social community.

One morning I gave my neighbour's daughter, a fifth form (Grade 11) high school student, a ride to school. Upon asking her what she was interested in she said she wanted to become a lawyer. "Oh," I said, "so you are interested in social justice?" "No," came the reply, "but the money is good." This child was embarking on prescribed a career path based on the criteria of monetary gain (not necessarily assured), rather than the sense of social responsibility that most clients would appreciate of a legal representative. For many professionals, the calling they answer is one of lucrative financial returns.

Many children who are wrongfully deemed 'not so bright', chase the same financial goals as my young neighbour, only to be confronted with limited opportunities and in desperation may turn to crime or become a solicitor of another type. Most of our islands' children, and the majority of adults I would suggest, go through life pressurised to chase set goals, and reach middle age with a sense of having missed something, of being pushed into a

The Nature of Belonging

life that hasn't been lived to the fullest. In our parental and social expectations (themselves prescribed), do we really understand our children or the needs of society?

The social problems that we share with nations throughout the world are not disconnected from our expectations of our children and call for us to review our commonly held assumptions if we are to respond effectively to the real survival issues that face us and will confront them.

Those who live their life on the prescribed path may be least adept at making this change. As much of their working life is spent ensuring that the track remains steadfast to their expectations, they will take few risks to jeopardize their career plan. When external factors present themselves to which they need to respond in a new way, they either cannot or choose not to. The very services and institutions that are set up to serve the public's best interests, may be more effectively catering to the career plans of individuals than empowering communities which beg for flexible creative responses. With their tracks firmly set turning centuries-old mental mechanisms, the personally ambitious cannot respond in full measure, nor will they welcome a fresh approach from someone who can.

So how are our immediate social challenges to be addressed? Could it be the ones who are not ambitious, who have not set themselves life goals, that are most adept at responding to change; who are more able to respond to real survival issues of growing food, being self and community-reliant, rebuilding bonds and community networks? Overshadowed as human resources they may be, but lack of ambition does not mean lack of a meaningful path in life. Their paths meander and flow, like a river changing course, responding to what is required of them. A rigid track of ambition has no time to engage in experiences in unexpected places, that feed an enquiring mind to grow wise. As a means of embarking on meaningful change could we begin to notice the existence of those we don't read about in the newspapers, who have not succeeded within the narrow definition of 'success'?

Because it seems to me that a sustainable future may be literally in the hands and minds of those embedded in direct experiences, who have no personal ambition but whose pathways connect them to their community and humanity at large.

May 2007

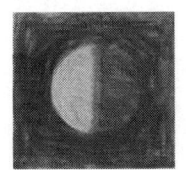

Mothers' Day of Healing

I was fortunate enough to be wished Happy Mother's Day by some of my students, which was much appreciated, though I always wonder how annual acknowledgement of this day impacts on our actions and responsibilities as the nation's mothers. Parenting is the most important job in society, one for which we are not thoroughly prepared. It takes years of training to become a lawyer, doctor, or architect, but we launch into parenting (a much more important job) without any preparation whatsoever. For some, a baby is an accessory or novelty; for others a burden. But there's no denying the enormous impact a baby has on her or his family and on the society- eventually becoming an adult capable of improving life for others, being problematic, or both. No child goes through life without effect, much of which is felt by her mother in untold ways.

Being a mother is an arduous and thankless task. As a single parent, I know the crushing responsibility and anxiety on a daily basis, of having to work and to provide daily care and control over children in challenging times. During a recent discussion with some of my students, the topic turned to their relationships with their mothers and guardians. According to some of them,

The Nature of Belonging

parental attitudes are either over-protective, or completely hands-off. In their experience, a child is either monitored to the point where they feel imprisoned or left to fend for themselves. Some of them are actually physically restrained. (Several students I have taught have been locked in rooms, and others come and go as they please with no questions asked.) According to the youngsters in the discussion, few parents are able to 'strike a balance' and they recognized that such extremes create emotional problems for the child and a sense of isolation.

The discussion increased momentum as the students became moved to express their feelings on such a sensitive topic. As I listened to their experiences, it occurred to me that both the over-controlling and the hands-off attitude reflect the parent or guardian's concern being more about themselves than the child. In both cases, the needs of the child are not met but the needs of the parents are, creating problematic children. Yet despite their own shortcomings, we hear parents readily complain about the younger generation.

Having identified these two extremes, the discussion moved to the question of 'balanced' parenting- how to provide the freedom to develop a sense of responsibility whilst, at the same time, provide the limits and structure that develops self-discipline. This is not just the challenge of mothers and parents but of teachers too. Either parent, particularly mothers, need a lot of support that is rarely forthcoming. The daily parental duties of being attentive to children; asking questions out of genuine interest (not intimidation); sacrificing personal desires to emotionally support; routinely cook, wash and clean, and help with school work without respite over a minimum fifteen-year commitment require the self-discipline and personal sacrifice that Mahatma Ghandi alluded to as the advanced training ground for women's spiritual fortitude.

As single parent mothers we are often blamed for the problems in society, which does little to effect change. Mothers are part of a community where they can be collectively supported rather than undermined by comparison and competition based on whose child does better than whose; one where all the children are loved as children of that community, not as children of separate families. Rather than targeting mothers for shame, recognition of the value of quality motherhood, through nurturing, support and encouragement can provide us with strength for our important job. Most mothers try, but don't succeed in providing for their children's needs, and feel isolated and unsupported.

Mother's Day, therefore should serve to strengthen us as mothers. We need positive reinforcement, energy, and support from extended family and community so that the sacrifices we make for our children can unite us, instead of dividing us through competition. Mother's Day should also heartily embrace mothers who have lost their children through gun crime, accidents, or illness. These women are coping with what must be the worst experience in life, outliving their child. The incidence of bereaved mothers is increasing at an alarming rate. They are feeling utterly lost and desperate and though their children have gone, their connection and love for them will never die. A mother's suffering is untold.

In our 'Happy Mother's Day' greetings, we must hold the hands of those who grieve for the remainder of their lives, for motherhood cut short, for as difficult as the day-to-day care giving is, the daily sense of loss is immensely more painful. In reflecting on motherhood, we recognize that parenthood is full of challenges for the children as well as the parents. How are we going to face these challenges with the composure needed to enable our children to grow into balanced productive youth who can answer to the call of their times?

Are we controlling them for our own ends, or are we giving them the support and encouragement they need to be able to contribute wholesomely to their communities? This is easily answered by looking honestly at our relationships with our children.

The Nature of Belonging

Depending how we express our love to them, their lives could hold change for the better, or suffering and destruction. They could commit violent acts, and they could be taken from us tomorrow. Whatever happens to them we should not blame children or their mothers, for mothers were once children too, many of them children themselves.

And like children, mothers need love and support. Happy Mothers are what we must create, not just a Happy Mother's Day.

May 2008

Message from the Sea Water Moon

The ocean weeps her immense
 body of wisdom upon our shores with glistening tears
    shed for
vanishing memories.
She rises up and swells with grief
            that mourns the loss of our connection.

She has watched her coastline
manipulated into the hostile partner that she lies with,
        until she no longer recognizes
her body contours,
pleading with the overseeing moon and sky
 that the mountain can lead us into trusting loving relationship once again.

'Mother is calling'
is the message in each mournful wave
        that breaks unheard against our altered shores.

6.

Mango Moon

June

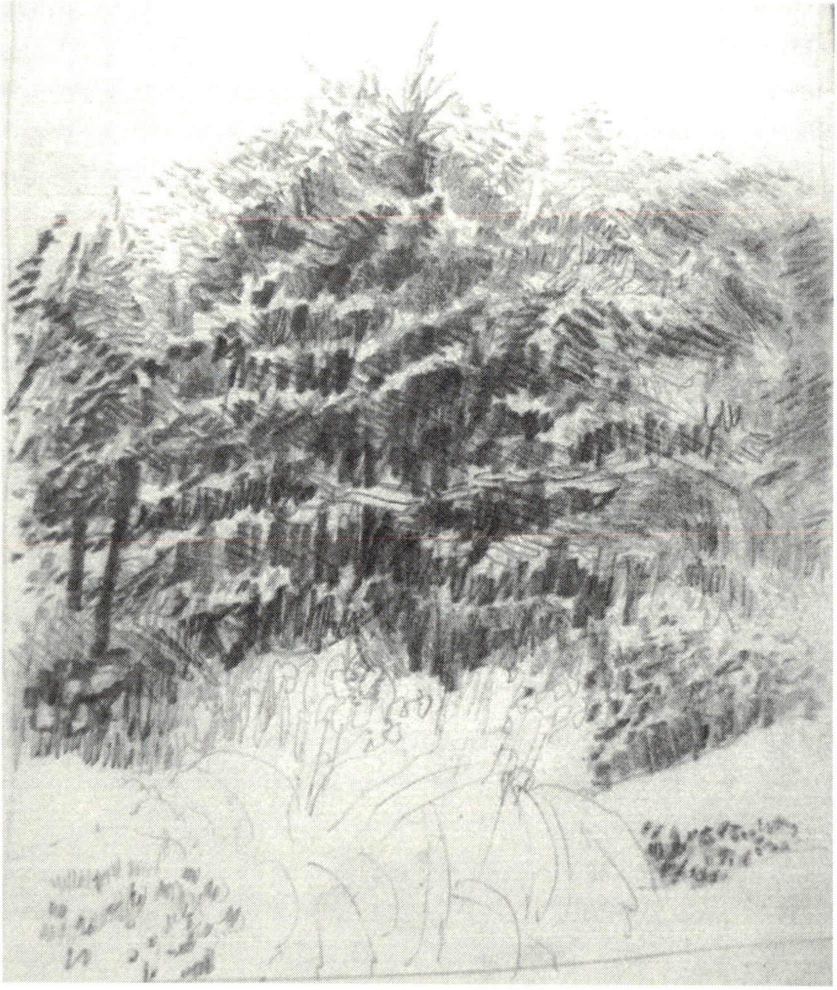

You are the light, I am the shadow. Here I can create supreme happiness

Healthy Common Sense: Virtuous Gardening

I have long been a proponent of growing our own food and the benefits of turning lawns into more productive areas by growing vegetables and fruit trees. But the delight of having fresh clean food to eat and share with others is only a by-product of having your own garden. In the process we learn about nature and the relationships between all living things through observation.

Sheep, cattle and other animals we see around us survive eating only grass and shrubs. Despite a limited diet they grow strong bones, muscles, flesh and fur. This simple observation tells us that everything we have to be healthy is already provided by nature, what's more it's provided locally. Our traditional heritage, a body of practical wisdom, grew through our ancestors' observation and contemplation of their natural environment. Great traditions and civilizations emerged from this simple yet profound act of observing, understanding and working with nature.

Yet, this art of survival has disappeared from modern day life, as we hustle and compulsively purchase, eat more than we need, specialize in professions, and become self-absorbed. The necessity to quietly observe and contemplate has given way to compulsive consumerism, a drug that we feel if we don't have, we will die. Yet the same substance that sustained and taught our forefathers is around us - our mountains and rivers, and the profound peace that they exude. What lessons can they teach us? One is that everything is interdependent. The mountains gather rainwater for the rivers that feed the sea, which in turn creates the rain in a continuous movement of change and exchange. This web of interdependency extends of course to human beings, but our modern day conditioning has blocked this understanding. Interestingly, nature does not depend on us; we could disappear and nature would actually be better off!

This should be a humbling thought for us- we are superfluous in the natural order of things- but then we must have a purpose. If this purpose is not to live in harmony with the rest of the living world, then we are truly a destructive, parasitic species. If you think my words are the ramblings of an artist with a passion for nature, then you'd be right. Since childhood days spent roaming the bush of West Africa, nature has never betrayed me. My life-long reverence for nature is creative and spiritual, but for others it may be just as importantly as a provider of food. We all relate to nature in different ways, some of us not at all. But a sad development of modern life is that we place little value on what nature can provide, which is considerable in terms of food, shelter and energy.

Fostering a positive attitude towards our local cultivators and agricultural entrepreneurs is as important as an appreciation for nature is; between them they provide local fruits and vegetables far superior in quality to what we import. Some who have lost their connection with nature may need facts to convince them about the nutritional benefits of foods grown locally in the Caribbean islands, and here some released by the Food and Agriculture Organization[18]:

-One guava fruit has four times the amount of fibre, and nineteen times the amount of vitamin C as an American apple.

-In comparison to a whole bunch of grapes, one guava has twenty-five times more vitamin C, four times more fibre.

-It would take fifteen American apples to supply the vitamin C content of only one West Indian cherry.

-Cranberry juice has become very popular because of its benefits to bladder health. Similar benefits could be had from coconut water at less than half the calories and with appreciably more potassium.

-Coconut milk, like the vegetable margarines is free of cholesterol. A tablespoon of coconut milk has only a third of the amount of calories of margarine. Also, coconut fat is healthier for the body than margarine fats.

-Callaloo (prepared from dasheen or tania leaf) has more than four times the calcium, two or more times the iron with more than twice the amount of vitamin A as the American vegetables such as broccoli.

-Compared to whole grain cereals our ground provisions are equally beneficial in providing dietary fibre. Our local breadfruit provides more fibre than rolled oats, or whole wheat bread.

But if this is not enough to raise appreciation for local agriculture, invest in your health through buying local produce and start up your own kitchen garden, next time you're tucking into a plateful of imported chicken, macaroni pie, rice, and potato salad, remember you can be eating cheaper and healthier from our local gardens. It's common sense, not the whim of dreamers, to live closer to nature, save money, boost the local economy and enjoy the benefits of better health.

April 2006

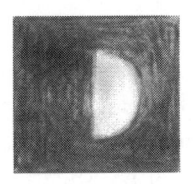

Graduates of Life

At a certain time of year, usually May-June, student graduation ceremonies take place at the levels of primary, secondary, tertiary and even pre-school education.

Every year, I proudly watch students from St. Vincent Community College as they graduate, particularly the art and design students who I have worked with since 2001.

The courage and dedication of those who persevered through numerous challenges has lead to creative and intellectual achievements and anticipation of future possibilities.

Many of the graduates return to our art room at college regularly. They interact with each other and are role models for other students in the programme. I help to keep them busy with projects of their own, and to assist with scholarship and job applications. This involvement in their lives after college has lead me to interpret graduation more as a beginning of their independent lives rather than an ending of their tertiary education.

Whilst the word 'graduation' carries the idea of commencement, its adjective, 'gradual', means changing or developing slowly by steps or stages. The moon above provides an exquisite visual reference for phases of gradational change. In art and design, the word 'gradation' is often used to denote the gradual and progressive change from one colour or tone to another. I teach an exercise that helps students to understand gradation, as an important practical concept applied to great artworks. The exercise involves shading a row of squares – from the white of the paper darkening each one slightly more until we reach black. The gradation is seen in a series of gradual stages of tones from the very darkest to the light- pure white.

This is a useful analogy for the meaning of graduation as the gradual movement along a path in incremental steps that, following one after the other, make the journey from dark to light. A graduation ceremony can be understood as marking one of these stages in life's journey. In this sense, we are all graduates of life's experiences. Our development and progress is not measured by ceremonies but by events and positive choices that move us forward.

For some, this graduation is seen as financial, heralding the stages of increasing wealth and accumulation. Those who seek power, measure their progress in stages of increasing influence and control over growing numbers of people or territories. But graduations measured in these terms are tenuous, prey to regression and have not proven failsafe in guaranteeing growth and improvement in personal character. Graduation really means 'progressive'- positively moving forwards towards the light- and when applied to life, can be measured in terms of inner work, improving our quality as compassionate and understanding human beings. Those who utilize their education and experience to develop and practice these qualities are the true graduates of life. Their development is of self and spirit, their progress measured by an increasing ability to give and to love, to help in the development of others.

If our young graduates can be taught this meaning of graduation it would reflect wholesomely on our national development. As future leaders and the nation's workforce, they would demonstrate less conflict and rivalry than their predecessors, and increased cooperation on a national scale would be the outcome of their developed consciousness.

The concept of graduation in education should not be confined to ceremonies but should be seen as instrumental in life, as revealed in nature's cycles. Whether we have had a formal education or not, whether we have reached secondary level or tertiary level education, we are all graduates of life.

Having applauded our precious youth in their achievements in school graduation ceremonies, as parents and teachers, we should applaud eachother too, recognizing that we are also graduates in the university of life. We are each our own best teacher and can regularly stop, assess our progress, qualify our direction in moving slowly, but surely and progressively, towards a brighter state of being.

May we major in peace, humility and compassion and may we all graduate with distinction!

July 2005

The Nature of Belonging

Wellness Grown at Home

During a period of months in 2007, we heard much in the Vincentian media about the 'wellness revolution' - a campaign that sought to promote wellness through healthy eating and exercise. But was it digested and excreted as another novel catch phrase that had no meaty substance? Did we assimilate any cultural nourishment from what was handed out?

I have considered the fact that the use of the word 'revolution' may impact our expectation of campaigns so-named. A revolution comprises transformation, not just an idea that becomes popular, or a slogan that creates an image of something being done.

A revolution always involves action borne of struggle that brings positive change to people's lives. In the context of some of our local initiatives the term 'revolution' might more aptly be applied after the desired change has come about and some other term coined prior to that. This may prevent possibility of great revolutionary movements throughout history being mistaken for mere 'campaigns' rather than monumental thrusts for human liberty.

Unfortunately the statistics at our health clinics, reflect a recent rise in diseases associated with an unbalanced diet as, due to food price increases, more poor people are consuming the cheapest foods in the supermarket, notably white rice, white flour and chicken back. None of which, we should note, are locally grown.

To have more positive and practical impact, the wellness campaign could be presented within the context of a 'homegrown' movement- where people are assisted to start (back) their kitchen gardens. A bi-weekly radio program with gardening tips, printed leaflets, and practical guidance from our graduates in organic agriculture returning from Cuba, could assist communities in self-reliance through providing some of their own basic dietary needs. Garden cultivation combines food production and physical exercise in one regular activity. Projects launched in schools across the nation could establish at least one or two organic gardens in every community. Such projects could be designed to integrate teaching subjects of social science, general science and biology at all levels.

A well-planned wellness campaign could also be a valuable opportunity for changing attitudes - such as the myths about coconut oil, and ground provisions being bad for health.

The commercial propaganda of the 1970s and 80s aimed to destroy competition for vegetable oil being produced in the US, and there are some people in my community who still believe that coconut oil is bad for health. They are eating a diet of unhealthy imported foods while the healthy foods that grow around them – ground provisions, coconuts, local fruits- go largely unutilized. We splash out on expensive apples and grapes unaware that a guava has multiple times the amount of vitamin C and is much healthier for growing children. There are countless facts to prove that a diet of locally grown foods far exceeds in nutritional content, a varied and expensive imported one.

A well-planned wellness campaign would involve transforming dismissive attitudes into appreciative ones for the farmers who are doing the most important job in supplying us with locally grown food. In the face of lack of recognition of the critical role they must play in sustainable development, they are a threatened human resource. The affinity born of productive interaction with the earth is our future and our past. As such farming presents a far more important contribution to national development than many sought after 'professional' practices. Farming encompasses a body of praxis that involves creating balance between variable elements, drawing upon all senses, not least of all, the art of observation.

Another science/art in its own right is the creation of healthy culinary delights. Most Caribbean people are artists with edible ingredients as their medium of expression. Creativity abounds in the kitchen and a wellness campaign could seek to develop this natural gift to benefit the nations health and creativity. There are hundreds of ways to prepare exotic dishes from locally grown ingredients that can enhance the traditional dishes. The excellent local recipe book compiled in 1999 by Dawn Smith for the O.A.S. Heritage Tourism Project, printed in St Vincent and the Grenadines, has simple creative recipes that are healthy using easy to access ingredients.

The building block of society is the food people choose to put in their mouths, because it creates the minds and bodies of those who build the nation. If this food is imported and unhealthy, then we should not be surprised at the outcomes- ill health, and lack of awareness about what is around us and lack of desire to use it beneficially. The loss of our own identity, I would venture to add, began with the imported food we put in our mouths.

Father Mark Da Silva, community activist living on Mayreau Island, remarked at a gathering in Kingstown in January 2009,."the Rastafarians are the only organized group since Independence who have managed to incorporate spirit as an essential part of their organization." It is well known that the strict 'Ital diet of Rastafarians comprises farm fresh local ingredients. Spirituality and food are not disconnected. Food creates our mental and physical energy as vibration, and as our Rastafari sisters and brothers know well. Methods of food cultivation and preparation create a mental, physical and spiritual connection with nature. With reverence to nature as the provider of our food (and shelter) we understand our own existence in relationship to her.

This living philosophy is far simpler, more practical and rational, more environmentally conscious than believing that money is our sole foundation and sustenance. We may struggle without money, but we cannot survive at all without food. Some of our own villagers living outside the monetary system are proof of this fact. Money in abundance does give us the power to buy novel imported food and products, but it does not necessarily buy us sound health.

Bob Marley sang "it takes a revolution to find a solution" and as yet, as is apparent by the clinics receiving new diabetes and obesity cases, we have not found a solution to unhealthy dietary practices and therefore there has been no wellness 'revolution.'

Despite the mass of information about healthy lifestyles on the Internet, (for those who can access it), and the examples set in our communities by centenarians and Rastafari families, our mainstream contemporary culture is based on unhealthy eating practices. Could this be partly because the alternative has a negative image: to eat 'local' is not in keeping with an 'upwardly mobile' image?

For genuine revolutionary changes to happen in our diets and minds, an awareness of the beneficial aspects of consuming home grown produce to our health and national economy must dawn. It most likely begins as we discover the joys and related health benefits of consuming home grown food. The revolution starts at home, with the natural food we put in our mouths, not the artificial words that come out of them.

March 2009

The Nature of Belonging

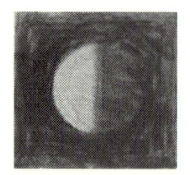

The Stately Kitchen Garden

There are many features that distinguish the middle classes' lavish modern houses in St. Vincent from the traditional style country homes. Many of the residential houses we see springing up creating suburbs are copies of North American style architecture. Their forms and plans are often sourced from the Internet. They are larger than is practical and tend to be hotter than traditional house, due to the position and style of the windows, and orientation of the house towards the sun.

Houses built up to forty years ago in our islands, were oriented relative to the sun's movements and biannual solstices, but now, we build without awareness of the earth's revolutions. The unnecessary clearing of trees from large areas of land so that a house may be visible is a reckless act on sloping land, creating potential for flooding and landslide and also contributing to the unbearable heat in some houses due to lack of shade. Many modern houses are not designed to suit our tropical climate, incurring extra expense to build and maintain. What happened to the common sense that only a generation ago, was a necessity of daily life?

Constructing enclosed spaces that are not comfortable to live in is an energy intensive use of (imported) materials and space that might be more productively utilized in outdoor areas. But there, outside the large house, we encounter another puzzling and fashionable phenomenon- the garden lawn. A favourite of the emerging middle classes, lawns are synonymous with social status; the more affluent the resident, the bigger the lawn. These grassy areas are purely decorative, non productive, and harm the environment both with the chemicals that are used to fertilize them and also with the clearing of trees and bushes, unbalancing natural ecosystems that provide for a diverse range of insects and birdlife. As lawns require constant upkeep by a gardener, they are expensive to maintain as well as being non-functional. Australian permaculturalist, Bill Mollison, states:

> "What we are looking at here is a miniature British country estate designed for people who had servants. The tradition has moved right into the cities. It has become a cultural status symbol to present a non-productive façade. The lawn and its shrubbery is a forcing of nature and landscape into a salute to wealth and power and has no other purpose or function."[19]

Mollison goes on to say that "lawns in America use more resources than any other agricultural industry in the world, they use more phosphates than India, and more poisons than any other form of agriculture. The American lawn could feed continents if people had more social responsibility. If the same amount of manpower, fuel and energy was put into reforestation the entire continent could be reforested. A house with two cars, a dog and a lawn uses more resources and energy than a village of 2000 Africans."

Being aware of these facts should make us think about our lawns differently and see the practical common sense of turning the lawn into a productive area of organically grown vegetables, fruit trees, herbs and spices. The lawn, or part of it, can be cultivated to produce for the household, and share with the gardener. Any surplus could be given away or exchanged with friends and we could enjoy better health by eating fresh vegetables, cutting down our food bills, and fostering community relations.

Better still, if residents with sedentary jobs, tend the garden themselves each day, they reduce stress and take exercise that might otherwise be conducted in an expensive gym. Outdoor activity can be shared with children, keeping them actively involved in the natural world and their local heritage.

Former Prime Minister of Barbados, Owen Arthur, relieved stress whilst in Office, by tending his garden every morning. It was an essential part of his daily routine, keeping him physically fit, reinforcing his character as a down-to-earth people's person.

As popular culture, gardens provide one of the most endearing features on the island of Dominica where houses have beautifully tended gardens, each one distinctive and unique. The creativity and resourcefulness of the people is expressed in their gardens that reflect the love for their homeland. The island gardens are personalized, reflecting the tropical bounty and rich diversity that is our Caribbean.

The imported suburban house and lawn have literally bulldozed away a traditional cultural Caribbean practice of organic kitchen gardening. Before too long we may see that it makes more sense to build smaller houses that are easier to maintain, just as we will be choosing smaller fuel-efficient vehicles. Those saddled with the responsibility of a large house, can at least do something about the lawn, designing it to be productive with fruit trees, vegetables, herbs and spices a haven for flowers, butterflies and birds, providing beauty in their lives and a daily fitness program. Those who are intent on having a large lawn around their houses should ask themselves why they feel it is low-status to make a productive area full of local character. The patch of soil around our house is our own canvas, giving us the freedom to express ourselves, our ideas and needs.

We could considerably improve our health, wealth and happiness, by entertaining a simple, practical alternative to the stress-laden responsibility of being fashionable.

April 2005

Message from the Mango Moon

As we give thanks for all fruits that nature bestows upon us, we consume in accordance with phases of life as they wax and wane from light to dark and back to light. By taking incremental steps we can regain our balance.

Our bodies will tell us when we have reached the good life.

7.

Creative Moon

July

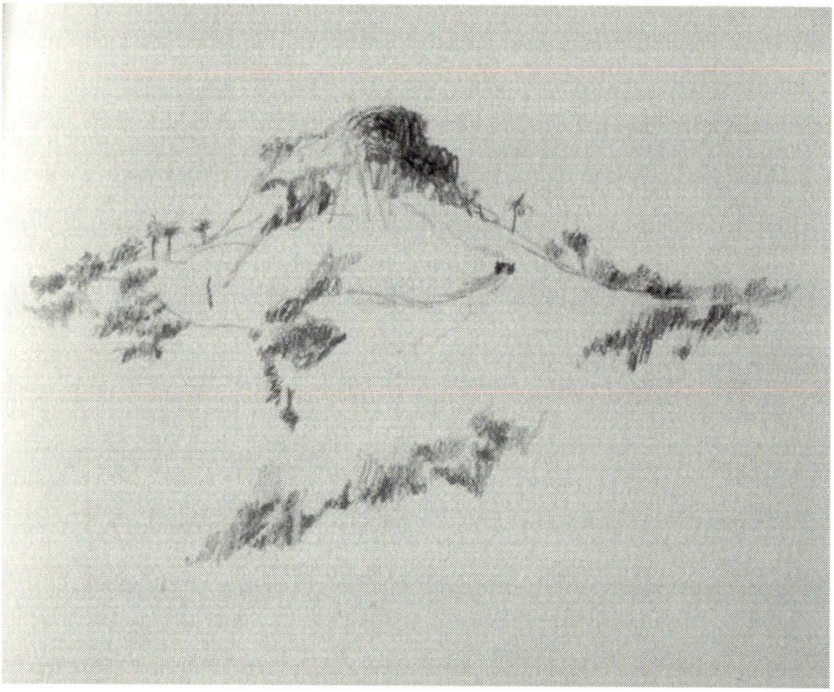

*To recognize one shadow-stitch in the blanket of life
is to know/feel what holds us together*

The Art of Carnival

That most extraordinary of Caribbean art forms, the Carnival, is no sooner over when the band leaders are formulating their creations for the following year. Some youngsters and I were discussing the topic of Vincy carnival and creativity when they stated an oft-heard opinion that there is formulaic repetition year after year in the music and costume designs. As they expressed boredom with carnival art forms, I suggested they should create their own mas' band, or collaborate with band designers.

My interest in Caribbean Carnival art began as a student in Manchester UK, when I undertook an aesthetic analysis in a dissertation on the costume designs of Trinidadian designer Peter Minshall's masquerade band 'Paradise Lost'. Subsequently, I exhibited hand-painted fabrics and costume designs in Japan and London that explored the theme of movement and dance as masquerade. Some years later, in London, I worked on theatre productions with Caribbean writers, and designed the set for Edward Camau Brathwaite's 'Mother Poem', into which I incorporated the symbolic use of masks. I later designed costumes, set and props for a touring musical production 'Glory', directed by Jamaican Earl Warner, which was set against the backdrop of carnival in Trinidad in the 1950s. In designing for that production, I researched Carnival from yet another perspective- that of ol' time mas'. The connections I had previously made between carnival and theatre were given the opportunity at that point to manifest through my design work. In this way, through an artist/designer's perspective, I nurtured a special relationship with this most extraordinary of art forms of the people. I came to view Carnival as an organism that has a life cycle. Even when not visible it is regenerating itself to reappear with indefatigable regularity. Like stage theatre, Carnival cannot be captured in a single static image. It exists within the audience's or performer's experience.

Carnival has erupted regionally as a unique art form that has engendered a number of professions and economic streams demonstrated by the introduction of a degree course at the University of the West Indies in Carnival Arts. Accredited inclusion into the educational machinery reflects governments' recognition of the art form's importance to the regional economy. Like theatre, Carnival is a synthesis of music, dance, written word, the visual arts, articulated through the collective creativity and aesthetic consciousness of the people. So, if many are of the opinion that Carnival has become predicable, what does this say about the society? Could it be that regurgitating the same forms with little variation or innovation, reflects the lack of creativity in the society? Has the focus for the Carnival organizers and artists shifted entirely towards commercialization, typical of other areas of daily life?

The observation that creativity is lacking in arts refers to an absence of progression or development of ideas, where the manipulation of composite elements (colour, materials, or audible elements of music etc) is formulaic, and expression does not vary noticeably from year to year, though the themes of the work may change. But even in the absence of innovative forms, Carnival remains an authentic reflection of the values our society. If it has become superficial and commercial, then the art form reflects a society obsessed with commercial consumer culture.

Whilst similar to stage theatre in some ways, the festival differs in that it comprises many events that take place, some simultaneously, in different locations. There are the shows of which we choose our favourites to attend: the musical components

The Nature of Belonging

of steel pan, soca, calypso; the costume bands that also have different forms, themes and sections. There are also many different types of visual art: costume, dance, performance, all distinct art forms that contribute to the carnival experience. Add to these many components, the variety of people that are attracted to take part from various countries and islands, and Carnival emerges as continually evolving, enticing returning nationals to set foot once more on their homeland to reacquaint and culturally regenerate. Although the kaisonians, and other artistes may prepare for months in advance, it's the ordinary people congregating, jumping up and revelling that bring carnival to life making it essentially a people's art form. The organizers can put everything in place, but without the people's animated participation, Carnival would not come alive.

The origins of Carnival are well known: a sedate, pre-Lentern street procession of the French plantocracy, was hijacked by the enslaved African population and an expressive, more vibrant carnival was born. Although society continues to evolve, carnival retains its importance as a social leveller and has been exported wherever Caribbean people have settled overseas. In the Diaspora, the West Indian carnival has absorbed traditions of other ethnic minority communities, enriching cultures, and fulfilling the basic human need for self-expression and a yearning for the homeland.

Meanwhile, here in the Vincentian homeland, where outlets for self-expression are limited, carnival provides an important opportunity for people to abandon convention and express themselves through legitimate channels. Recognizing that carnival began by fulfilling a psycho-social need and continues to do so, we should examine what role it is playing for us in St. Vincent and the Grenadines today and how we can develop it.

Contemporary Carnival has become increasingly commercial as a money earner, through the ticketed shows, the manufacture of costumes, corporate promotions and street vending. But the shift of emphasis from communication to commercialization (and on the importation of materials), belies the traditional spirit of Carnival that was concerned with creating out of what was available. Originally, Carnival exemplified recycling through the utilization of discarded materials into art forms. This process drew on the ability to see familiar things in new ways and reinterpret them as a catalyst of the reveller's creativity. Nowadays, apart from some remnants of the J'ouvert procession, we pay to join a T-shirt band or wear a costume made from imported materials. A creative avenue, heaving with ideas from the masses, has been abandoned for impersonal profit-driven Carnival production.

But are there other ways that Carnival can benefit our society besides as a money earner?

An authentic art form communicates original ideas and messages, and has meaning besides the expectation of exchange for money. The original people's Carnival revolved around the experience of freedom accessed through creative expression. Caribbean people are inherently creative and feel that Carnival can generate this creativity through its various art form components to the benefit of visitors and locals alike. An aesthetically robust Carnival would also favour improved commercial interests.

My suggestions for strengthening the creativity element of Carnival start with recognition of the potential social and educational through Carnival arts:

a) A study could be conducted by the SVG Carnival Development Corporation into the educational potential and benefits of the Carnival Arts, to identify linkages that could be made to existing curricular learning programmes in primary and secondary schools. Working through the schools would have positive impact on the studies of various subjects as well as initiating more Carnival-related activities in outlying communities.

Carnival makes an excellent theme for a coursework project; educational programmes can be introduced in various subjects- history, social studies, geography, art and design- whilst children learn about their local heritage and culture. I also suggest that a new post of Carnival Arts Education Officer should be created within the CDC or the Ministry of Education, with the specific responsibility of liaising with schools, facilitating school/community partnerships and developing Carnival education resources; and researching areas of good practice in the development of Carnival and Carnival arts in schools.

(b) A Carnival Arts Education Network, could be established which will act as a forum for information exchange, partnership and curriculum development between teachers, academics, carnivalists, libraries, schools, community groups, musicians and designers.

(c) The creation of Carnival Schools' Competition for school-based Carnivals could take place in the communities. This would have the effect of developing creativity and environmental awareness through teaching about recycling materials, also reconnecting with the tradition of carnival, and building community ties.

The suggestions I am making are not just about improving Carnival- they are about using Carnival as a means to improve quality of life by developing our creativity through communal action, creating awareness of our culture and environment, and building community spirit, which has declined through urban migration and other factors such as introduction of cable TV. Practical steps of this sort could result in a more dynamic Carnival art form, and could develop the most distinctive and original of the small island carnivals, the basis of a successful marketing strategy.

Carnival is an evolving art form that breathes its people consciousness. It lends itself to many different creative possibilities and interpretations, and to enhance its creative content, we can guide the process of its development towards fulfilling a need for cultural, educational and social enrichment, from which economic benefits will inevitably follow.

August 2004

The Nature of Belonging

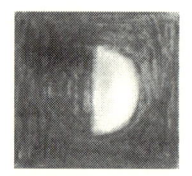

You Can Eat Culture!

Cecil 'Blazer' Williams' words of appreciation for those present when the New Artists Movement (NAM) paid tribute to his contribution to cultural development in St. Vincent and the Grenadines, revealed the dilemma of the conscious artist in contemporary Caribbean society. Blazer disclosed that had he been able to glean financial support from his writing and theatre directing he would not have taken up a profession in law. His statement belies a sad fact- the reality of an artist whose full contribution to developing a thriving national cultural economy has been compromised.

That's not to undervalue Blazer's formidable contribution through his writing and plays, the production of which was only made possible through his ability to create and produce after work hours and through the understanding and tolerance of his family. We should not underestimate his contribution over the years, but neither should we underestimate the creative heights he could have taken others to, had the institutional support been there for him to utilize the theatre to its full effectiveness in public education and community consciousness building. Had NAM been given full support at governmental level, we may have had by now, after twenty-five years of the group's inception, dancers, playwrights and performers throughout the schools; a younger generation more aware of social and environmental issues through the transformative powers of drama in schools and communities. Blazer's words resounded with the grief of every artist who feels the pain of thwarted creativity: "Cultural expression is self-development, it develops organizational skills, community awareness, and enriches the life of the people. The politicians do not understand or appreciate this vital importance to nation building.

In fact culture is seen as a sort of side show instead of an essential ingredient or force in the development process."

A famous quote by a local politician, "You can't eat culture," reveals the establishment's ignorance of the potential of the arts in generating livelihoods and national development. The word 'culture' originally means, "the planting of crops and the tending of animals". According to this definition, you can indeed eat culture, just as surely as one can earn a living from cultivating original creative expression. But, like many other truthful realities and possibilities hidden from us throughout history, the truth about culture was suppressed to keep the strength of our inherent creativity at bay, to ensure repression, for it was known by those who dominate, that cultural expression is the key to mental liberation. The sovereign power of expression is inherent in blues music and authentic J'ouvert masquerade and other forms of cultural assertion from within the plantation.

Cultural expression manifested as reproduction has fallen prey to the erroneous notion that we only live through materialism, that the spirit does not need feeding, and if we suppress the carriers of culture- our artists, our women, our youth - we can effectively starve the spirit. And, without spiritual strength, we are easily satisfied with a diet of consumerism. Sustainable economic development can be built on culture as it relates to creativity and production. The tourism industry is a prime example of a market dependant on cultural forms.

A report by the Caribbean Development Bank in 1998, identified the main constraint to the development of the tourism industry in SVG as the lack of an art and craft market.[20] Barbados' Minister for Trade and Industry Reginald Farley at the opening of the Caribbean Craft Market place in 1998, stated that the "success of the tourism industry in Barbados is measured by its handcraft

The Nature of Belonging

sales." Productive and utilitarian arts can also generate income in design fields of graphic design, fashion, jewelry design, interior design, household accessories, eco-architecture, landscaping and many more viable and necessary professions.

Gross attitudes of colonial domination fed us the lie that we cant eat culture, which we swallowed, heartily washed down with an abundance of Eurocentric tastes, that set the standard for art and for beauty. Such a toxic consumption was kept down with overdoses of rote learning at school, which removed our ability to question and, coupled with deprivation of creative education, quenched any flicker of doubt that the Eurocentric values are superior to anything local. But some artists, poets and writers survived this cultural poisoning and their destiny as a result of their questioning has been made even more grueling -they were shackled and dispensed of through accusations of being abnormal for not having swallowed the lie and choosing in their 'madness' to live off culture. The stranglehold not only compromised the work of individual artists, but also deprived the whole society of its creative legacy, robbing our youths of their cultural inheritance, of a sense of direction and belonging; of their roots.

Blazer is a genuine artist who could not wholly stomach the lie, having nurtured the creative spirit of NAM for over twenty-five years. We can no longer remain ignorant about the role of our society's cultural creatives in this era of the 'post colonial' economy. At the Caribbean conference in Washington in June 2007, Barbados' Prime Minister Owen Arthur said, "We have to create and sustain open, rather than closed systems at both the social and economic levels to generate new opportunities and bring the marginalized into the mainstream of social and economic life."

The marginalized are the poor, the women, the illiterate, the youth and the artists; the artists in all of them, the capacity for creative thinking in us all. Can we bring these into the mainstream of social and economic life? To pave the way in these critical times, we should liberate our artists, secure scholarships for them to further their studies, and at last instate creative development as a general function of education and a necessary force in the development process. Then the legacy of Blazer's work and that of other eminent creatives will not be lost to society, nor confined to limited circles of nostalgia. For as an enduring artist, he knows that cultural expression does not belong to any one individual, but feeds, nourishes and prospers the entire nation.

A Mindless Feast?

Carnival season is the ideal time to review many social practices, which during this period are thrust to the forefront of everyday behaviour. One such practice is the portrayal of women and the internalization of their role as sex objects.

Carnival promotes a concentration of images of women as mindless sex objects, whose credibility is based on whining credentials. Women themselves actively promote this image onto our sons and daughters. Whilst a supple waist may well be one facet of a woman's endowments, at Carnival it is magnified to the extent that it surpasses all others.

Such rigorous annual conditioning reinforced by all-year advertising campaigns has created a socially acceptable expectation of women and young girls as primarily providers of sexual thrills and entertainment. The majority of our women and girls have been subjected to the humiliating demands of this expectation and females falling short can expect ridicule, rejection, and even threats in settings ranging from the workplace to the street to the bedroom. When the abrasive Carnival atmosphere dies down, the perception of women as sex objects, albeit slightly diluted, is left in its wake.

Should we be surprised by an outrageously high incidence of sex crimes when we are openly cultivating such attitudes?

If we examine the origins of Carnival as enacted by enslaved people we find no evidence of this denigration of women. In the West African Yoruba tradition from which many islanders descend and many of our cultural forms originate, such as calypso, ole time masquerade, elements of language, culinary arts, the qualities admired in women were courage, determination and clear headedness. Women were expected to hold positions of leadership.

The traditional European view of women is domestic, voiceless, disfranchised and essentially subordinate to men. As we emulated Eurocentric culture our image of women changed. Ironically, whilst the majority of Europeans now find this attitude totally unacceptable, we obsessively reinforce archaic prejudices from colonial occupation.

Seeing life from only an economic and political point is a manner of perception that is similarly restrictive. This perspective has not only hijacked the essence of Carnival, the largest festival in Saint Vincent and the Grenadines, but the entire entertainment industry. It has infiltrated our minds to create a hostile environment for creativity and critical consciousness.

But who is willing to disembark the wagons of frivolity and return Carnival to meaningful national expression? In June 2009, against the backdrop of Carnival activities, the work of a group of twenty women artists and poets came together in one space under the collective theme 'Seen AND Heard'[21]. The audience ranged in age between 8 and 80 years. All who heard their words and saw their images were inspired to have hope through the positive energy rarely seen nor heard in our communities, dominated as they are by violence and enslavement of our minds. Their diverse voices came together with a determination that made grown men in the audience shed tears in recognition of the unspoken voice of their mothers, and the spiritual strength and unity of women that enables our men to achieve.

The creative action of women forms a critical foundation of cohesive social relationships, without which we cannot develop and heal our wounded communities. Women's creativity can heal us as a nation. The creativity of a woman means providing the love, skills, guidance and environment to express our own thoughts, whether through words, images, movement and music,

The Nature of Belonging

masquerade, or through community action. Until we place women above the monstrous barbarism of male chauvinism, we will never understand who we are. Our female poets and artists, who articulate a diversity of perspectives, wrestle on a daily basis with imposed demands conflicting with their inner voice. Some of these women draw support from conscious brothers, in their courageous belief that they are worth more, much more, to society than fleeting entertainment.

Will courageous women be regarded as freaks or will their voices be heard, images be seen and messages be digested as transformational and healing remedies for a society that wallows in a mindless culture? If this question, posed in the midst of carnival activities, seems out of place, contrary and even disruptive, then the answer is a resounding 'Yes, the creative thinkers are freaks'.

And hence the unique festival that once provided a life-line for an honourable culture, instigated by those regarded as 'freaks', today provides more for reckless consumption of what oppresses us.

July 2009

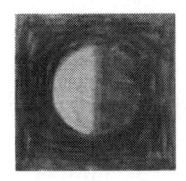

An Empty Cultural Package

The term 'cultural industries' that we have accepted unquestioningly, like much else handed to us from the industrialized north, bears some examination in terms of its effect on our perception and expectation of the creative arts sector in a small Caribbean island.

Marrying the two words 'creative' and 'industry' is ominous from the standpoint of an artist and creative educator, whose priority is to nurture creativity as a highly sensitive, complex and insightful process culminating in purposeful work.'Industrialization' implies mechanization and repetition through mass production. Is there anything industrial about a small island's creative sector or its local culture for that matter? Do we really want to industrialize creativity- a process that will relinquish original expression for formulaic representation? Has industrialization not invariably destroyed authentic cultural expression- and indigenous culture? Are we dealing with a contradiction of terms and action as banal as implied in the term 'spiritual industries'?

Of course when we talk about industries we refer to economics, so 'creative industries' refers specifically to the economic value or commercialization of creative products. Whilst we need to foster this value to the benefit of the nation's economy, we also need to be aware of the power of language to mould our perception. If we think of culture and the arts only in terms of earning power, we reduce our art forms to shallow replicas (already happening) and forsake the creative process through which great art works are made. The Caribbean Regional Negotiating Machinery Report of 2006 "Cultural Industries in CARICOM" states:

"The cultural and creative sector refers to aesthetic, identity and copyrightable goods, services and intellectual property. It embodies a wide array of activities that make and circulate sounds, words and images or a combination of the above. In short, the term cultural or creative 'industries' describes the economic activities of artists, arts enterprises and cultural entrepreneurs, for-profit as well as not-for-profit, in the production, distribution and consumption of film, television, literature, music, theatre, dance, visual arts, masquerade, broadcasting, multimedia, animation, fashion and so on."

We know through our own experience as well as what the report states, that creativity, ideas and artistic skills have economic value. But the germination of ideas through which these skills flourish, comes through circumstances that are removed from the intent of generating income- they come initially through the will and need to express. For instance, the first group of youths who began beating steel pan in Trinidad, in its original form as a discarded oil drum, were not thinking about how much money was to be made from the only instrument created in the 20th century. It is practically certain they didn't make any money from their genius. Similarly, the hip-hop artists felt their truth and spoke it from the street long before they reached recording studios and mega stages. Bob Marley's protest songs were written in the ghetto to uplift the spirit of the people, through lyrics of hope and dignity. It's important not to lose the essential value and function of creativity whilst focusing on its potential economic value, which is a by-product of authentic expression founded on the reality of people's experience and spirituality.

Many creative thinkers in the region see the preoccupation with modern industrialized concept of development as destructive to authentic culture.

Industrialized development has become synonymous worldwide with wasted resources, environmental destruction and the annihilation of intangible culture. St. Lucian visual artist and poet, Adrian Augier, uses the metaphor of the polar bear sitting on a melting ice cap to illustrate the effect of modern development has on our culture. He sees people in the Caribbean islands drifting apart as their culture melts away. During a symposium at CARIFESTA X, I raised with him my discomfort with the two words 'creative' and 'industry' sitting side by side, and he agreed that it is another example of how we in the islands accept terms and terminologies from outside without thinking of the impact on our minds and spirits. He added, however, that he thinks we can create our own interpretation–that "Caribbean people have a history of using foreign symbols to represent something else that started in the plantation." The fact that we may still have to resort to this tactic surely implies we are still in the plantation. At what point in our cultural realization will we repossess rather than be obliged to represent?

At the same symposium, Gladstone Yearwood, Director of University of the West Indies' Errol Barrow Centre for Creative Imagination, advised us to proceed with caution with regards to the 'creative industries'. His concern was that to have an economically vibrant creative sector in the Caribbean, we must not lose sight of the creative process. He observed that the artists, who should be at the centre of the thrust for development of the creative sector, have been left out. Trinidadian artist Mikemba Kunli made a similar point the same point:

> " the possibilities for creative education are ignored whilst attempts to package it continue until it has no meaning."

Professor Yearwood reflected that CARICOM governments recognize the importance of infrastructure for tourism and other economic activities -international airports, ports etc- yet fail to put in place equivalent for the cultural activities-galleries, museum, tax rebates for innovators, import duty concessions on materials and equipment. The nurturing of creative process also takes place through systematic arts and cultural development plans in schools and communities.

Professor Yearwood believes the cultural sector "must move from lacking integrity to being organized in such a way to empower people, from producers to consumers, to connect the Caribbean Disapora" and for us to own the models and systems of production and distribution.

So whilst the catch phrase 'cultural industries' has caught on without question, can we create our own words and descriptions, express our own experience? Can we listen to the artists who struggle to articulate but who are denied validation, even as their governments discuss the development of 'industries' based on their efforts- artists who are not included in the discussion or decisions, yet are expected to produce and perform, without participating in the process that moulds their destinies? Is colonial history being repeated as we attempt to build industries on exploitation?

The major role of the Arts in society is as a catalyst for change, yet we seem to be getting more of the same.

September 2008

Message from the Creative Moon

Art is production- the outcome of the creative force that we all have, consciously directed through media and materials. Art as production may not transform the society, but creativity can, and the production of art and design, can be a catalyst and measure of not only the transformation process, but of the consciousness of the people.

By not enquiring as to its extraordinary nature, we have packaged our creative force for convenience and commercial duplication. Treated thus, it has diminished in our midst to formulaic repetition. Those who contain the creative force, our women, are similarly packaged as novelties.

We could make much more of what we have by enquiring: 'What exactly is it that we have got, what makes us beautifully strong and powerful?'

And with an effort to bring back, to fertilize the growth of consciousness, we expand to mine the depths of creative Belonging.
What treasures we uneARTh !

8.

Mountain Spring Moon

August

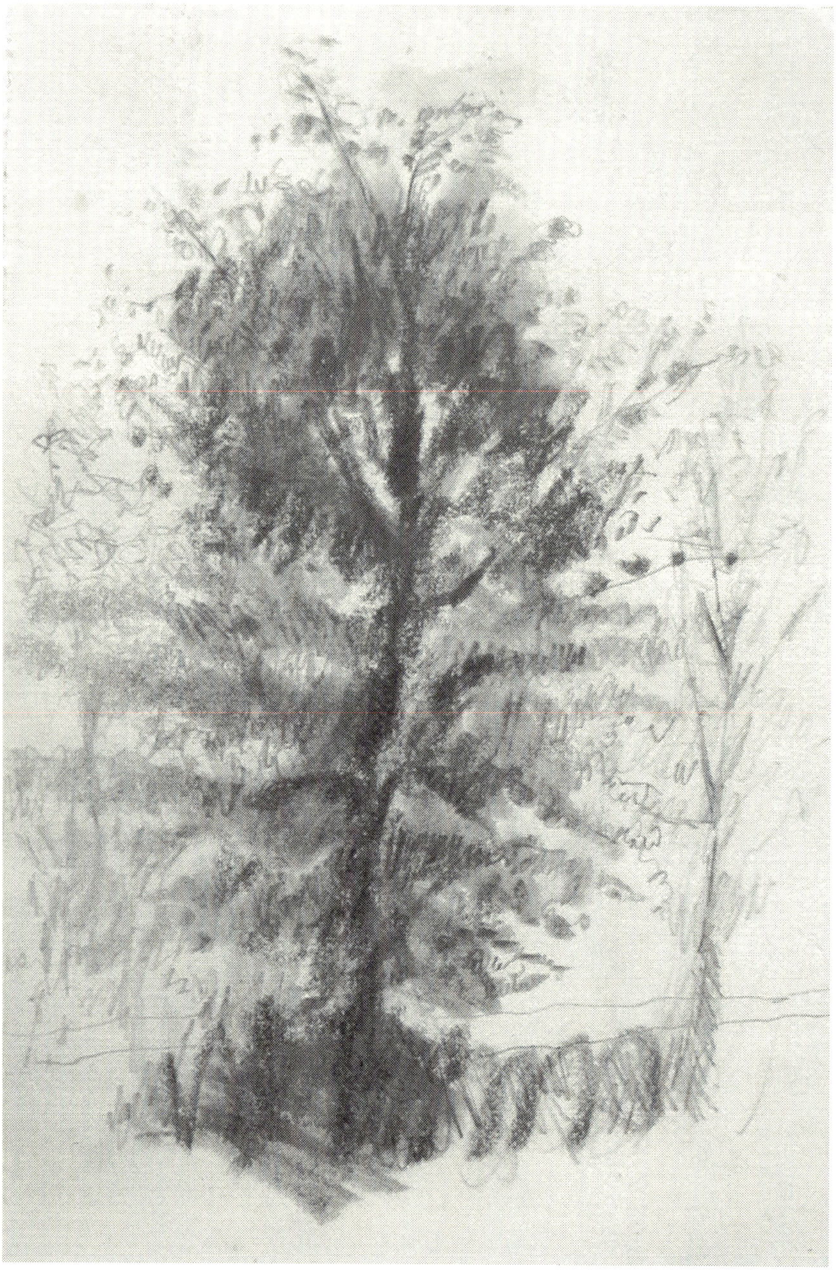

I saw the leaves dance with delight. I saw joy in decay and the completion of nature's cycle.

I breathe the clarity and wisdom of the forest.

The Nature of Belonging

None But Ourselves

The importance of Emancipation Month is well-recognized in Caribbean islands, but how effective are the celebrations in developing our consciousness as a free and independent people? Did emancipation, in the true sense of the word, really take place, or did the passing of the Emancipation Act of 1833 merely signal the passage of the oppressed into a more politically correct presentation of oppression; into a modified system of slavery that would continue to serve the interests of the colonial powers?

After emancipation, the instillation of fear in the minds of the enslaved did not disappear but its methods of enforcement simply changed from physical abuse to the inculcation through an altered employment strategy and through the education system of the Imperial Policy. I recall a lecture I attended in 2003 by foremost Caribbean novelist and cultural critic, George Lamming, where he said that freedom cannot be *given* because that is where we start. He stressed that "we must be careful what we are celebrating because the people who passed the Emancipation Act did not have the victims' interests at heart." Lamming went on to explain the meaning of the word 'emancipation' which literally means 'to take out of the hand'. Continuing with this metaphor of the hand as the imperial power, Lamming said, "Although enslaved people moved from being *in* the hand, emancipation represented their being taken *out of* the hand but not out of *control* of the hand." Emancipation celebrations, he said, should therefore, "celebrate the struggle to break the hand"- he believes, as yet, we in the Caribbean have not broken the hand.

If our focus on emancipation is to impact positively on our developing consciousness, we should contemplate the immense struggle of the victims of the hand, a struggle expressed through art forms in the music of resistance; a language of resistance (creole); traditional mas'- a physical expression of liberation, and many other important skills of independence, notably natural farming and healing arts that sustained families and whole communities. The substance of the lives of those who created these forms must not be lost, for it contains the essence of authentic Caribbean culture. We should learn by reflecting on emancipation, that history is constantly in the making by the daily lives of ordinary people, not only those who have political power.

The hand of imperialism creates mass dependency through generating needs, fears and prejudices that destroy true cultures and inhibit development at all levels. The same hand that oppressed the enslaved continued its agenda through an education system based on authoritarianism and subordination, which successfully inculcated several generations, but is failing the majority of today's youth. Modern cultural imperialism has overwhelmed us through the TV and in particular the American soap opera, (which Lamming claimed over ten years ago as the main contributory factor to the erosion of Caribbean culture.) Economic imperialism is evident in the flooding of the market of imported goods that local producers cannot compete with, and in export strategies dictated by industrialized countries.

Slave owner Willie Lynch, predicted in 1712 (documented in the Willie Lynch Letter[22]), that the psychological control mechanisms of slavery would last for 'at least 300 years,'- a prediction that manifests in our readiness to be engulfed by imported cultures and practices, materialistic values and destructive environmental practices of industrialized countries, without contemplating the long-term effects on our fragile island ecosystems and economies. The accessible path to improve the quality of life for the whole society long term is obscured in flooded markets competing for our attention. Independent thought and action, needed to follow

The Nature of Belonging

that path, is generally deemed troublesome and unwelcome. (This is particularly apparent in the class room/workplace where creative thinking is in conflict with the general idea that a good student/employee does not question what the teacher/boss says; they achieve promotion by subservient repetition of information, yet may not have an original thought of their own.)

Self-organization, creative thinking, fresh ideas and new hope cannot grow in institutions that function as conduits of imperialism. In the words of Paolo Friere, a Brazilian democratic educationalist, "it is incredible to see how black people were and continue to be so prevented from being."[23]

The hand of imperialism takes many forms and this is why Lamming warns us to be careful how we celebrate Emancipation. True liberation, that he defines as "a sense of spiritual connection to the landscape and an inner sense of independence as a manifestation of freedom," will become apparent first through the arts, concerned as they are with self-determination and a sense of being and identity. Despite the slave owners' agenda imposed three hundred years ago, many of our ancestors rose with dignity through the humiliation of enslavement. The power to resist mental subjugation through sharpening of the creative imagination was the legacy they left us. Celebration of Emancipation can embrace a legacy constructed from their lived experience and realities, as well as their African heritage.

During Emancipation Month we should ask ourselves the question, "Have we learned from the legacy of our fore-parents - would they be proud of us today?" With our minds still in the grip of the hand of imperialism, maybe they would not. They may urge us to free ourselves by trusting our own experience, and to express it with conviction through what we do.

Bob Marley must have heard the echo of their thoughts when he sang in his Redemption Song, "None but ourselves can free our minds."

August 2004

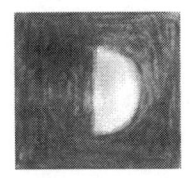

Champions of Integration

In the month of September 2004, two phenomena swept through the Caribbean unifying people in the various islands. The first, a natural disaster named Hurricane Ivan, and the other, the victory of the West Indies cricket team securing the Champions Trophy- their first major tournament victory in 25 years. Both events created a sense within all English speaking Caribbean islanders that they belong to a wider territory than their own single island and that they are connected with others across the sea.

The lasting jubilation that the victory of the West Indies cricket team, brought to many people across the island nation states, can hardly be matched by any other human accomplishment. It was the central topic of discussion throughout the islands for days afterwards and the ensuing sense of pride will live on in the hearts of Caribbean people for a long time to come. The record breaking partnership between lower order batsmen Browne and Bradshaw, symbolizes the strength and determination that Caribbean people can apply in times of crisis, when all appears to be lost. This accomplishment was all the more poignant for people across the region struggling desperately to rebuild their lives after Hurricane Ivan ripped through our territories.

During the historic match, images of the jubilant and demonstrative West Indian cricket fans living in Britain flashed across our TV screens. The unification of Caribbean people through the West Indies victory embraced those in the Diaspora, celebrating through sport their enduring connection with their homeland. Sport has enormous influence in creating connections

The Nature of Belonging

between people from different and distant geographical localities as every islander can relate to the cricket team as their own.

In what other fields of endeavour is a Jamaican proud of the achievements of a Barbadian? Or, put another way, how else can what a Barbadian does, uplift the spirits of a Jamaican? Separate islanders commonly feel like foreigners, sometimes adversarial, towards each other. Only through sport, music and natural disasters do they demonstrate evidence of a strong cross-regional resonance, transcending boundaries and uniting our spirits to recognize what is the truth of the Caribbean community - a range of peoples whose diverse traditions, in which so many of them have their origins, their memories, their hopes, are bound together. The capability of sports to unite us, as seen and felt clearly in the case of the endeavours of the West Indies cricket team, is matched by dance and music expressed in Carnival arts which have been exported to countries of the Diaspora. Sports, like the arts, inspire unfulfilled potential to aim for goals that may start as possibilities in the imagination. Involvement in sports and arts cultivates strong characters, leaders and high achievers; people who do not give up.

So why are sports and arts the least developed subjects in the education system when, apart from the power to unite, they are the most effective subjects in teaching life skills such as communication, group cooperation, organizational skills and creative thinking?

As a tool for regional integration, sports could be utilized much more effectively through the formation of teams that represent the region, as well as national teams. Despite the existence of an Organization of Eastern Caribbean States sports desk, squash is the only sport represented in the Caribbean region by an OECS team where players from several islands make up the senior and junior teams. Friendships and business connections are made through the interaction of players, tournament organizers and spectators from different islands. Other sports should be encouraged to follow the example of squash and cricket. The latter, with a Windward Islands and West Indies team, is the pioneer of island integration through sport. Other team sports such as football, netball and rugby are represented internationally by separate island states, as is athletics.

We have seen how well Caribbean athletes, particularly sprinters fare in the international arena- wouldn't these accomplishments benefit the entire region by competing as the OECS or the West Indies? In the case of football, a regional team would be far more competitive in the world cup. If we cannot see the benefits of having more regional sport teams we should ask, "What would have been the chances of the Windward Islands cricket team bringing home a victory over England?" No doubt there would be challenges in managing regional teams, not least of all the cultivation of inclusive team spirit. But the benefits to the entire Caribbean should provide ample incentive to work through these challenges as the West Indies cricket team exemplifies.

Sports and the arts, apart from having the potential to deepen regional integration, are key elements in developing a sustainable tourism product. From fostering individual pride and inspiration, providing careers, boosting national economy through impact on productivity and tourism, to engendering kinship between islanders, the cultural sector is central to the healthy functioning of any national economy. The Caribbean community extends far beyond the islands into pockets of the Diaspora. However long they have lived abroad, West Indians, including those born overseas, will always support the team from the motherland. The intangible bond through the distance is born of and strengthened by cultural expressions that create a collective emotional experience. This is what binds us to the home island, and to each other, far more effectively than imposed economic, commercial or party political loyalties. (It is no coincidence that we have seen cultural forms utilized to underscore the latter.)

With more effect than preaching the importance of unity as an abstract concept, practical undertakings in the fields of sports and arts can engage us on our home turf and reach out to the Diaspora.

The Nature of Belonging

Once thus engaged, economic benefits and cultural exchanges would follow through sponsorship and patronage without overt persuasion. The optimum outcome of the employment of sports and arts in individual nation building as well as regional and international relations, will be achieved effectively if grounded in childhood experiences. Every village needs its own playing field and hard courts for ball games to organise inter-community tournaments, to encourage the talents of the youth to find an outlet through physical expression. Every school needs a vibrant arts and sports programme. Sports and the arts are indispensable in preserving heritage by counteracting the negative forces of imported culture, lessening the incidence of drug abuse and violence among the youth. This, plus the obvious benefits to general health through an active lifestyle, would significantly reduce government expenditure on medical services. (Some of these funds could be utilized in training instructors and creative educators.) Surely these social benefits, apart from the far-reaching economic ones, provide ample reason for our governments to promote sports and arts in schools and beyond.

The benefits of such commitment are obvious, from fostering individual pride and inspiration, to improving levels of mental and physical health, strengthening communities, boosting national economy through impacts on productivity and tourism, and fostering kinship between islanders. From the farmer in the field to the barrister in his New York office, across conflict-ridden and insidious social divides of material wealth, political affiliation, racial and cultural backgrounds, all of us united in the victory of our cricket team.

This is a declaration that the achievements of our sportsmen and women, artists and musicians should not only be regarded as commercial opportunities, but as catalysts for community connection and national identity. Having direct experience of the power of these forms to unite, there is no reason for us to hesitate in taking the required steps to develop the enormous physical and creative abilities of our people. So close within reach, these steps are fundamental to paving the way towards economic and political recovery and to engage the spirit of a people without which our society will remain divided.

A natural disaster and a sporting event have been seen to unify our people, in the last month- one through the necessity of overcoming great turmoil and suffering, the other through collective effort and accomplishment, the source of collective elation and pride.

On the path to regional integration and more productive societies the politicians and policy makers would do well to pave the way through sports and the arts. We can then be proactive, not dependent on a disaster, to unify our people through enhanced latent abilities.

September 2004

The Nature of Belonging

Message from the Mountain

Recently in Kingstown, I allowed myself a few moments to sit and contemplate a scene from the window of the Bounty Café in Halifax Street. I noticed the mountain standing serene behind Dorcetshire Hill that towers over the town. In the foreground people were hustling back and forth, some with cell phones clutched to their ear, oblivious to the beauty and even the existence of the majestic landscape behind them.

I thought how starkly the scene throws into contrast the opposite approaches to life: the mountain embodying the natural, peaceful, grounded, and the cityscape, which is artificial and fraught with activity. The city has pulled us from our mountain homes, and changed our lifestyle into one that ignores, then forgets, the landscape from which we came. The mountain is inescapably part of our island heritage; its rivers feed the ocean and its earth once fed its people. Island culture grew from the hills and mountains, the Garifuna ancestors sought refuge in them; they nurtured whole communities.

The mountains form not only the visual drama of our island, they are the source of life's essential element- water. They generate the volcanic soil that Vincentians are proud to say is among most fertile in the world (unfortunately no longer true). But the erosion of the mountains and depletion of the earth is of no concern to us in the city; we pay the mountains little attention as we absorb ourselves in progress, as defined elsewhere.

My life-long fascination with the mountains started in Africa as a child. I have lived amongst or close to mountains on four continents. As a teenager I hiked the highlands of Scotland, the Cumbrian Lake District and the Welsh peaks. In Japan at university I lived in a teahouse in the mountains surrounding Kyoto for two years. More recently I have travelled to the Andes of Venezuela and the mountains of Colombia and Dominica.

But the mountains of St. Vincent have been my home for seventeen years and are amongst the most beautiful that I have known. They have drawn me into their peaks and mystical forests for days at a time, to observe and experience the mountain drama that is the intense peace and power of nature. Trees and plants survive based on extensive life support systems. The intricately balanced ecosystems that once covered the entire island, have now retreated to all but a few mountaintops. The sight of our unique squawking parrot flying overhead has, in our charge, become endangered as only 700 now remain in their natural habitat.

I wish to share my most treasured mountain experience with all Vincentians, because it is part of them, of all those connected to these islands through birth or residence, through family at home or abroad, to appreciate what has become merely a backdrop to our city- and to share the beauty of the mountains we see but seldom acknowledge.

Our obsession with city values of power and politics, our social status, the annual shopping frenzies have construed to divide us. The model of tenuous progress we follow, teaches us to judge eachother on our appearance and the number of our possessions, not on the quality of our character. We buy into the constant human drama without question, to feel more important than our sister or brother. All this means nothing in the mountains, the staple of our heritage and culture. In the cradle of the landscape we are all one, nature does not create senseless divisions between us. We could open up our lives to the mountain message of liberation through progress of growth based on nature's living systems of self-organization, through interrelationships and networking, flexibility, diversity, interaction, where everyone, every element plays a part.

The Nature of Belonging

Last time I descended from the mountain I wondered how many more years will it be before our eyes open once again to Nature, our greatest teacher. On my return I was appropriately greeted by this message from a friend in New York that read:

> "My Friend this is a reminder to celebrate all the things that are good in your world… The people you love, the places you love are a part of the memories you hold onto, and those unforgettable moments when you close your eyes and breathe in life with a smile. I hope your heart is filled with lots of little reasons to celebrate each day."

That message made me realize a lifelong reason I have to celebrate is that I have known the mountain.

I hope we all have reasons to celebrate the simple pleasures of life and not become overcast by lofty aspirations of a fabricated world. Our small island reasons to celebrate, embodied in the air we breathe, the earth beneath our feet and the mountains that remain, however much we disrespect them, the reference for our collective Belonging.

December 2006

Filed Away Where?

In the summer of 1993 Dr. Adrian Fraser, Director of the UWI Centre for Continuing Studies, asked me to conduct a summer art camp for children in the old Grammar School sixth-form annex building, Kingstown. Fifty-six children attended between the ages of 6 and 12 years.

I was to learn very valuable lessons from that short but memorable experience that prompted me in turn to ask many questions of the place that was to become my homeland, St. Vincent. The experience was to develop a clearer understanding of the function of creativity in society and was pivotal to my later commitment to dedicate more time to creative education than working as a freelance artist/designer. This commitment was consolidated through close observation of indicators of inherent creative ability in our children that reminded me of the boundless expression of aboriginal secondary school children I met in 1987 in Western Australia.

I witnessed the Vincentian children, similarly accept creative tasks with joyful abandon. Every morning the art camp started with group exercises, which, after a few days, the children took turns to lead, with pride and responsibility.

The theme I chose for the camp was 'water'. Through various activities we explored the water cycle in nature, systems of transportation, conducted basic scientific experiments, made musical instruments and model boats, sculpted sea creatures. We explored through poetry the powerful water imagery of Vincentian poet Owen Campbell's 'Washerwoman'. The art camp

The Nature of Belonging

programme thus encompassed all subject areas- science, social sciences, language arts, physical education, history, visual arts, music and dance.

Being my first time working with a group of children (my experience lecturing in two arts universities in the UK, did not prepare me for this challenge), I was somewhat overwhelmed at first by its large size. To make it more manageable I created 6 smaller groups and endowed each one with the name of fish- sardines, jacks, tuna, sharks, dolphin and parrotfish! Although this was initially devised to spare me having to memorize so many names, the children loved assuming an adventurous identity in a shoal instead of being dispersed as individual competitors. A sense of camaraderie and belonging quickly formed among them. They were so absorbed in the activities that only one incident of unruly behaviour occurred during the entire workshop.

Those youngsters are now between 22 and 28 years old and I have heard several of them reminisce about the art camp experience that, in relative time, was just a speck in their childhood, but was experientially much larger. Some received their first creative experiences within a collaborate environment and their artistic interests were fuelled, (some to be sadly suppressed later on).

In response to the unquenchable creative spirit the children demonstrated, I subsequently ran Saturday creativity classes for three years in the Cotton Ginnery building, Frenches, Kingstown. Years later some of those students years arrived at the A-level art and design programme at Community College, providing me with the precious and unusual opportunity to work with a child in their infancy and adolescence. It was in that first workshop that I saw something so convincing I could not ignore: the powerful expressive energy in children of a society that bafflingly provided few outlets for it, little encouragement and even prejudice towards its development. I questioned the foundation of a society ignorant of such a tangible force to harness for productive action in all areas of national development, and in that ignorance construed to stifle its most precious resource.

I was aware, having young children of my own, that arts and sports were not given significance in the school curricula. The reverence placed from Grade 1 on repeating information for the reward of marks and class positions, still culminates in the worship of a tortuous 'common entrance' examination that further compounds social hierarchy and division from the age of 11 years. Arts and sports are effectively marginalized through underfunding. Art, and its even more stigmatized partner, craft, are regarded by administrators and the general public as 'hobbies', not even granted the respect of being termed 'visual' or 'creative arts', appropriate to a robust multi-faceted subject leading to practical professions, some of which had forged my livelihood as a freelance artist/designer. In those early days, I detected among administrators, that my passion for creative development as a general function of education, was regarded eccentric and rather amusing, the reflection of a whimsical mind. I was, like the subject itself, a bit of a joke and stigmatized accordingly.

I am still deeply perturbed by the social implications of an institutionalized education process so far removed from the understanding Albert Einstein accumulated over a lifetime when he wrote:

> *"I am enough of an artist to draw freely upon my imagination. Imagination is more important than knowledge. Knowledge is limited. Imagination encircles the world."*[24]

Einstein knew, through his own experience, that the creative imagination is indispensable to great scientific and artistic accomplishments. The loss of 'self' during the creative process which Hungarian Psychologist, Mihaly Csikszentmihali, refers to as 'flow'[25], enables an affinity (empathy) to develop with our environment and with others, and thus creative education produces more compassionate individuals.

Professor Rex Nettleford, vice chancellor of the University of the West Indies, was to highlight the importance of this to

The Nature of Belonging

a Kingstown audience at his lecture in 2008, when he said that Caribbean societies must move from "individual opposition to collective participation and collaboration." Such a shift may seem momentous, but I had seen the summer art camp children move from nameless individual strangers to happy members of a group (a shoal of fish) in an instant, and the outcome was the production of some intellectually and artistically sophisticated work.

But whilst children respond to change rapidly, it seems that adults have a lot of catching up to do and languish in their social response abilities. Albert Einstein also remarked:

> *"Significant problems cannot be solved at the same level of the thinking which created them."*

So, if the problem is the demise of youth potential, unresolved by the failure of authorities to respond by urgently redesigning an outdated colonial education system that remains aloof to the needs of the child, then it must be the youth themselves who bring a new level of thinking to provide the solution.

The demystification of the technocrat's job may not sit comfortably in the swivel chairs of ministerial offices. Some may scoff and resist facilitation of simple, practical possibilities, based on observation of the child her/himself. Yet what I observed happening in the summer art camp of 1993, was a healthy response of students to connective experiences for learning and expression that every child deserves to have throughout their formal education. A love of learning is fundamental to a child's confidence, productivity and fulfilment throughout life. To encourage them to question fosters a creative attitude that engenders more love in an ever-expanding heart.

Many significant social problems we face require revitalized thinking to solve, but from where will original thinking arise if not from our boundless creative resource that brings hope, compassion and active involvement? Ignorance of this fact finds more expression than creativity in our shameful blaming of the youths for their negative attitude. Having blocked their ability to be productive, we then blame them for what they have become! This demonstrates the limited comprehension that created the problem and explains why simple solutions within our reach have proven elusive- community arts and sports centres; effective art and sports programmes in schools; community playing fields, where youths with energy and frustration can find outlets physically through sports or emotionally through the arts. It takes a simple mathematical calculation to reveal the correlation between lack of such facilities and incidence of violent crime.

During painful years of seeing the exceptional creative ability of our children and knowing much of it would be thwarted, hope has been reinforced through the determination of many youths, among them the extraordinary achievements of St. Vincent and the Grenadines Community College Art and Design students.

Assisting them in their realization is not glamorous amidst creatively disabling attitudes. I have been at times barely tolerated for possessing the conviction that they are capable of much more than formulaic repetition of second-hand knowledge. For believing, without doubt, that we have a cultural endowment of emotional intelligence, of creative imagination that pre-empts all great discovery.

I cannot dispense with such a conviction to comply with social norms, formed as it was from an intuitive knowing and qualification of my own creative path. I cannot replace what I know within my heart with a cold framework of rationale that contradicts my experience, to betray my life purpose and that of our children. I cannot replace ancestral life source with the processing of mind to conformity. For I have all that I need in the breath of life itself and in the collective realization that our children express with such joy and freedom when given an enabling environment. They are, as nature intended, all we need to study for life's most valuable lessons. If we watch and listen to them we will know how to proceed. But to perpetuate our treatment of them in ignorance of life's treasure is to bring utter misfortune upon our communities. We are currently witnessing in our population the physical, emotional and spiritual effects of neglect of the creative imagination.

> *"Nothing in the human psyche is more destructive than unrealized, unconscious creative impulses... When it is a question of a mass psychosis, nothing but new, creative conceptions, brought up from the depth, can stop the development toward a catastrophe."*
> *—Marie-Louise Von Franz, Jungian analyst.*[26]

Von Franz echoes Einstein's belief that solutions must emerge from an alternative approach to problem solving.

In a breath of life our infants become adults and we adults become elders. In adulthood, children will express what has been done to them, through how they choose to live. Having everything we need in nature and our hearts, can we cease to thumb through the files of technocratic obfuscation and grasp the opportunity to create for our children simple, local experiences of self-realization, of emotional completion and environmental reconnection?

September 2009

Message from the Mountain Spring Moon

As surely as the sun sets and rises, we are born and we will die.

Our death begins not with the onset of old age but with the slavish indoctrination of information designed to coerce us into compliance with material self-interest, but in reality prevents us from knowing ourselves, understanding our children and living peacefully with others.

9.
Bountiful Moon

September

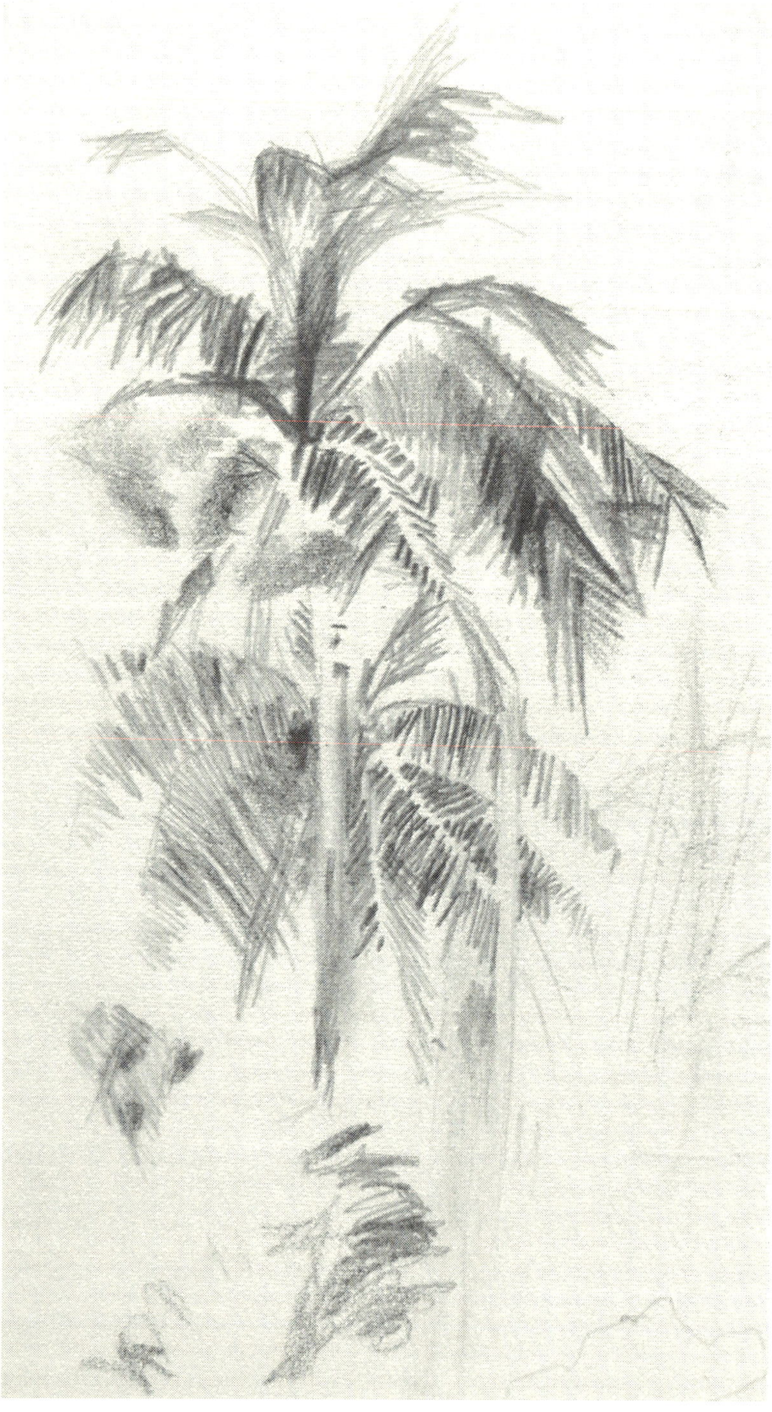

*They spoke of days gone by,
of hands that toiled while nature looked on.
They spoke of shadow gifts
[of countless lessons unlearned]*

A Modest Culture

Many people in our Caribbean islands are lamenting the demise of the agricultural sector, a sign that people are realizing that, as agriculture disappears, we are losing an inherent cultural connection, a part of ourselves that relates to the landscape.

But agriculture has, in our misguided progress, been pushed aside to make way for an imported development model based on high-end tourism, informatics and offshore banking. I'm sure we will live to regret this thrust because with it comes many social problems borne of the neglect of the human spirit and a preoccupation with profit and greed. With it we remain in the grips of controlling foreign driven forces that are exploitive and have no interest in the empowerment of the people, or what the islands can produce for themselves. Given the profit-driven politics of corporations and the historic grooming of our political systems into similar devices of persuasion, the ordinary people themselves may be the only ones who care about their own empowerment. Suppressed through an education system that creates mental dependency and a political system with a rational of domination, the people have no confidence in their own culture, of which agriculture plays a central part. But we will discover eventually that these humble practices that came out of ordinary peoples lives, now frowned upon, are indeed our most precious treasures. Traditional farming is one of these practices, a national treasure, and one of great value to our development.

It's true that agriculture as we have come to practice it, with expensive imported inputs, has become labour intensive and

The Nature of Belonging

financially unrewarding for the small farmer. These difficulties are nothing to do with the art of farming itself, but the methods we slavishly follow. Using expensive artificial inputs has created a dependence on a certain way of doing things, leaving us with a limited perspective of farming and where the soil has not been washed away, it's far less fertile than what we started with. These artificial methods are not sustainable and totally different from traditional farming, which worked with principles of nature, not chemicals. If you doubt the wisdom of traditional farmers then consider why when Europeans arrived in the Americas they found the soil rich and healthy even after 50,000 years of use by the First Peoples. And yet after a couple of generations of tilling by the Europeans, the soil was turned to sand.

Sustainable agricultural practice rebuilds the soil naturally with layers of organic matter, so that it constantly regenerates itself. With this method one-quarter acre can easily be managed by one person to feed two families. If this sounds revolutionary or outlandish, picture the rainforest where nature, left to its own devices without the interference of man, is abundantly lush, supporting a totally harmonious living ecosystem. Trees and plants thrive with no fertilizers or sprays, no slashing or burning. Trees of all species and sizes live harmoniously. In fact they all depend on each other for their wellbeing, growing mixed together as they do, they attract birds, butterflies, creatures above and below the soil.

What is happening in the soil of the rainforest is of particular interest to natural farmer/gardeners. It regenerates itself through dead organic matter forming a mulch or layer over the surface. This retains water and breaks down into nutrients for the plants. It is a natural system of feeding the plants and microorganisms in the soil. Agro-forestry and natural farming are based on studying this natural system and reproduce it for productive agriculture. Many farmers throughout the world, in Mexico, Cuba and Japan fro example, have adopted natural farming and are producing yields equal to those produced using chemicals. I myself am practicing these methods and enjoy an abundance of produce for the household. The soil is not dug or turned, but mulched using organic matter from the land; fruit trees and vegetables and herbs are grown together; green manures are planted, that is plants rich in nitrogen that can be cut and left to decompose into the soil as natural fertilizer. The system builds a beneficial community of crops, not a monoculture. As in the rainforest, there is no soil erosion in natural farmland. Pests are kept down by growing other plants that deter them and by mulching with cuss cuss (vetiver) grass. The culture attracts beneficial insects.

So I would ask, why are we following expensive, artificial models of farming when we have an alternative? Natural and organic farming practices can feed local populations and produce sufficient for export, whilst reclaiming our soil and forests in the process. Agricultural tourism, would bring in foreign exchange and strengthen our local culture. Natural farming is part of our culture- those traditional farmers who fed their families from a small patch of land understood the wonder and complexity of nature before they replaced tried and tested methods and natural wisdom, with chemicals and artificial farming. So what are the specialists and agronomists doing? Young people return to our islands from Cuba with qualifications in organic farming but where is their knowledge being put into practice?

No wonder we are in a sad state, feeling that our very survival is threatened. Turning our backs on nature, we have lost our connection with our spirit that even in their darkest hours, our ancestors managed to retain. And a loss of spirit has dreadful repercussions: the corruption of values, as greed becomes the new development model.

Today the general public and even the farmers themselves are being convinced that agricultural land can be put to better use for luxury tourism or housing developments than for food production. This is the kind of propaganda that makes Japanese natural farmer Masanobu Fukuoka outraged. He believes that agriculture must be made a foundation for living and that the future of a small island lies in the hands of the farmer.

I agree with his view especially when he says "A culture born of human recreation and vanity that is divorced from nature cannot become a true culture. True culture arises from within nature and is pure, modest and simple."[27]

April 2006

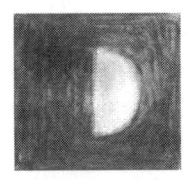

Food: Activism or Praxis?

CARICOM governments met at an emergency meeting at the end of 2007 to try to work out a common approach to food prices. The question of high and rising food prices is behind the spiralling cost of living from one Caribbean island to the next and is a real challenge to contemporary living. According to Trinidad and Tobago's Daily Express, food prices constituted the number one issue for the people of Barbados as they prepared for a general election; food price-led cost of living is causing havoc to household management from the Bahamas in the north to Guyana and Suriname in the south.

Prime Minister Patrick Manning made food prices his government's number one priority outside of high and rising crime. At the meeting, CARICOM leaders pledged some swift action, both in terms of identifying a list of food items which will be studied by a team of experts for purposes of reforming the region's Common External Tariff, and in identifying the export and import capabilities of member states for those goods. At the meeting the Guyanese government offered to make a portion of its considerable land space available to other member states in CARICOM for productive use.

Meanwhile here in St. Vincent, Renwick Rose, Coordinator of the Windward Islands Farmers Association (WINFA), recommended a comprehensive approach to address the availability of food by putting food security in a wider context of that of 'Food Sovereignty'. In his weekly column in the Searchlight Newspaper, Mr. Rose defines food sovereignty as "the right of people to define

The Nature of Belonging

their own concepts of food and agriculture to determine the extent to which they wish to be self-reliant in food production, to assume control of their resources, agricultural land and sea."

We hear and read about tackling the food issue on regional and national levels, both of which require bureaucratic meetings and legislation. But there's also a personal approach to the issue, which in my opinion, actually determines the others- that is, the personal relationship with food in our own lives, in our daily culture. This impacts on and determines all these other food issues. And whilst we hear a lot about food prices, food security, food as nutrition, food supply etc, we don't hear about this important aspect of food as culture. This has two meanings: food as cultivation, and food as part of daily culture and custom. Food is culture in the sense of being central to survival, but at the same time is a form of cultural expression and manifestation of the identity of a people.

The culinary arts are a valuable form of aesthetic (artistic) culture. In a very real sense what we eat makes us what we are and determines what we are capable of. Food affects a person's physical and mental wellbeing, therefore impacts directly on the health service. Food holds families together, or disperses them as the case may be. Attitudes towards food reflect social status. Obtaining food is the preoccupation of poor people; lack of access to it the cause of many disagreements and escalating civil wars.

We can easily conduct a visual analysis of the food we consume as a nation. A look at someone's plate reflects who he or she is, what their values are, how they view their own health, even the extent to which they are in control of their health. The majority of Vincentians eat mostly imported food most commonly bread, chicken, rice, macaroni pie and potato salad, made from imported ingredients. Wheat and rice do not grow in the climate in which we live, and are therefore not culturally appropriate staples for our bodies.

A cultural revolution could occur if we simply base our diets on what grows locally. Through increased demand we would create more income for local farmers and could cut our food bills further by reviving the kitchen garden that was common up to ten years ago.

We are living upon what was a fertile earth and one that, using natural farming methods, could be fertile again. What is more central to our culture than eating the food that grows out of that same earth? By eating what grows from another soil we are literally putting another culture into our veins. This cultural transfusion, imparts degenerative diseases. In consuming imported food we also consume lashings of fossil fuel energy that runs the machinery for processing, packaging and transportation causing the high prices that will continue to escalate as oil prices rise. By neglecting to aggressively promote local produce and sustainable farming, our governments are major instigators of this cultural transfusion. Food as imports are slices of prices and profits, subsidies, tariffs and taxes, but the real facts of food are in our minds and bodies, in the choices we make to eat what we eat. And we do have the power of choice.

In St. Vincent and the Grenadines, most people have a natural gift for planting and growing. People who possess such skills are the most resourceful people on earth. Why has this gift of inherited practical knowledge and wisdom become as neglected as the land itself? Why has what many Vincentians do best been forsaken for dependency and financial expense and ill health?

So while the heads of government try to find solutions through beaurocratic channels, why are we, the people, not being practical? We surrender our very existence to others when the answer, or part thereof, is lying right outside our doors in the space in the yard, in the gift in our hands and the will in our minds. No solution could be more readily presented to us.

Our reluctance to create food, to restore yards and lawns into productive supply is simple proof that imported culture has consumed us. That we are no longer connected to common sense reality, seduced by advertising and follow-my-leader mentality. On regional, national and personal levels we remain mentally enslaved by imperial forces, but through the practical acceptance of food as culture in our own yards and from our own farmers, we could unite and free ourselves from this vicious cycle of history.

Let Food Sovereignty reign free - for a truly prosperous sustainable future, let's resolve to eat what we grow and grow what we eat.

January 2008

Farmer in the Diaspora

On an airplane from Barbados to London one July, I was fortunate to find myself sitting next to a gentleman from Layou, St. Vincent, a former mason and farmer called Ephraim Simon. I was reading a book on the journey, "The Road Back to Nature" by Japanese farmer, Masanobu Fukuoka, and Ephraim's interest in what I was reading caused us to strike up a conversation from which I learned a great deal.

Ephraim was born in Layou and had lived the past eight years in London. It turned out that he had lived most of his adult life with people well known to me in my community of Penniston. With his relatives there, he farmed the lands for years in the mountains of valley where I live and in which I also farm. We thus had plenty to talk about, especially a shared love of nature, the valley and village life.

"The Road Back to Nature" struck me as appropriate to Ephraim's life, having lived most of it in nature and now living removed in an impersonal culture in the big city. Ephraim, like most Caribbean Diasporans, was happy to reminisce about home and the days when he lived a simple but wholesome life in St. Vincent. He spoke of the peace he felt at the riverside and a powerful sense of connection with the mountains and the whole of nature. He reflected on the quality of blue light that hovers over the hills at full moon and of the majestic views through the rolling valley to the sea. He spoke of the colours in the sky at sunrise and how he once lived with a sense of belonging to the earth.

The Nature of Belonging

Ephraim was describing a strong unbreakable, multi-sensory connection to his home landscape that many Vincentians possess and become more aware of when they move overseas. They adopt a new life in the UK, in Canada or America but never fully belong there. They continue to yearn for home and can cannot find replacement for the peculiar and unique quality of Caribbean island life. This is particularly intense for those who lived connected to the landscape, which constitutes a deeper understanding of island culture.

Ephraim described his routine and isolated life in the city of London as: "people move from home to work and back again, interacting with nobody, just earning money and paying bills." He said that there is no 'true nature' there, and that even the greenery in the parks doesn't feel natural. His four weeks' holiday every year is spent in his beloved St. Vincent visiting friends and family in the island, where nature is still evident even though it is fast disappearing.

Eventually Ephraim asked if he could borrow my book to read on the journey. After reading for a while he pointed out a section of the book that read, " far from being able to observe the real state of nature and grasp the essence of God, man only moves further and further away from nature and God." Ephraim was visibly moved by what he read, concerned as it was with the spiritual in nature; it resonated completely with his own perception and experiences as a farmer in the Buccament valley.

We eventually landed in Gatwick airport and caught the train to London. Having not visited the UK for several years, I felt awkward and unfamiliar with the surroundings; the redesigned airport layout was a culture shock for me. Ephraim, the farmer from Layou, helped me make a phone call, buy my train ticket and assisted me with directions.

When we reached Victoria station in London, my son came to meet me, and with thousands of nervous commuters he and I scrambled on to the underground train service, just four days after the July bomb blasts. The first train we alighted was evacuated after a security alert, which was to be a common occurrence during my stay.

Meanwhile Ephraim had gone his way on a similar tube train journey to his London apartment, and amidst the alien city pressure I reflected on how fortunate I was that my time in London would be much shorter than his; I would soon be back in our beloved mountain land, the St Vincent he dreams about from a distance and whose landscape spirit he carries in his heart.

He is among thousands of other Vincentians who have relocated abroad, and have acclimatized to a culture without nature. Their yearning for the homeland is an invisible part of Vincentian culture resonating from the heart and minds of many thousands who have left its shores for the dubious attractions of big city life. Materialism and higher salary, are trappings for which a much higher price is paid – the price of belonging, of connection and all those things Ephraim spoke about.

Those of us who remain on the island are caretakers of a precious island landscape legacy, tragically unappreciative of what is in our midst as its natural beauty disappears in the race to become a modernized, unsafe alien culture. Our development involves not working to preserve nature but dominating and destroying it.

As we replace local culture with an alien one, we will eventually experience a sense of longing like Ephraim; but we will pine for our own island culture without ever leaving its shores.

August 2005

The Nature of Belonging

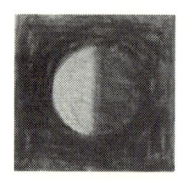

A National Living Treasure

Among many extraordinary people who live in our valley community, there's an exceptionally wise one, Mr. Lawrence "Captain" Guy residing in Top Village, Vermont.

Mr. Guy originally hailed from the neighbouring valley of Marriaqua. As a young man, he crossed, on foot, the mountain that divides two beautiful valleys and descended into Vermont.

I was introduced to Mr. Guy some years ago by Micky Kirkwood from Queensbury who had met him as a child when Mr. Guy worked for his grandfather, John Punnett. Micky lived overseas for many years, before returning to reside in the valley of his childhood whereupon he reconnected with Mr. Guy. Their ensuing meetings were to flourish with shared memories and laughter and opportunities for Mr. Guy to shine in his role as brilliant storyteller. The ample showering of homemade treats helped in no small measure to enhance these celebrations of enduring friendship. Micky was inspired to being collating Captain Guy's stories and the personal history of a man with a lifetime of rich and varied experiences.

After being employed by Micky's grandfather, Captain Guy worked for three of his uncles. His vivid recollections of those days, retold in his masterful way, would create a living context, to mesh with Micky's own childhood memories, and reinforce his conviction that he was back at last in his true home. Such a strong sense of valley belonging that defies verbal definition, can nevertheless be effectively expressed through skilful storytelling accompanied by gesture and expression, a glint of the eye, all joyfully employed by Captain Guy as means of sharing life experiences that have inspired him into a productive old age. I feel fortunate to experience such informative and entertaining visits to Mr. Guy's home, highlighted by his captivating smile and irresistible culinary treats.

Capt.' has the appearance of a person in his late 60s but he doesn't mind me disclosing his actual age of 90. Having read about centenarians in Dominica and Ecuador, I was particularly interested to see if the factors identified there – diet and lifestyle – also contributed to Captain Guy's youthful appearance and attitude. A first glance around his house and garden confirmed that, yes; he definitely has a healthy diet and a physically active life.

He maintains a lush quarter acre garden that provides a variety of fruits and vegetables, herbs and spices. He has a chicken pen, rabbit hutches, work shed, all designed and hand built by himself, finely crafted and neatly kept. He has acquired abundant knowledge of traditional cuisine through processing cassava farine, arrowroot and cassava starch, cocoa, preserves and sweets, and fruit cordials. He makes flour from a variety of tubers and fruits- sweet potato, green banana, breadfruit, cassava, tapioca- that he dries and grinds in a hand-mill or on any one of his collection meticulously hand-punched zinc graters. He explained that the idea of making flour from breadfruit occurred to him when wheat flour was in short supply and he noticed so many fruits wasting on the ground during the prolific breadfruit season. His solution was to make flour, which stores well and makes a much healthier alternative. He now is embarking on a project to demonstrate this process from harvest to the finished product.

Mr. Guy's resourceful activities extend even further as all his life he has survived through his knowledge of traditional culture. As a youth, he apprenticed as a lumberjack and carpenter, learning his first trade from his father in Mesopotamia. A sought-after coffin maker, Capt. crafted the coffins of many departed valley dwellers, including that of Micky's grandfather. His skills in construction have been put to use building many styles of house, including the one he presently lives in, for which he felled the trees and cut the lumber himself.

During the Second World War, he narrowly escaped death on precarious journeys by boat to and from Aruba. His heroic actions at sea earned him the nickname 'Captain'.

Back in St Vincent, he managed various areas of Cane Grove and Queensbury estates in the 1950s-60s, whilst engaging in his own farming ventures. He's also an accomplished canoe builder, with intricate knowledge of the forest. During his travails at sea, he also learned how to sew and knit.

Such vast and varied experience, adventures and breadth of knowledge, establish Captain Guy as a man of unparalleled wit and intelligence, of awesome practical skills. He tells us his range of skills was once commonplace but are now rarely found in one individual. Such skills are inseparably part of his daily life and the basis of survival, and obviously the key to a long healthy life and youthful appearance. With the disappearance of these skills, the stories based on a multifaceted connection with experience and a creative attitude, powerful stories of a vibrant culture, are disappearing along with those who live to an advanced healthy old age.

As I sat in awe of this national living treasure, I pondered on how valuable knowledge is no longer preserved through daily life practices, that daily culture has undergone such radical change as to render skills of self-reliance as unimportant. The community network that passed such skills from one generation to another has disintegrated in modern life.

Mr. Guy has expressed sadness that the youth he has encountered are not interested in learning practical skills of how to grow food, how to build and make things. He is desperate to pass on his knowledge as he realizes its value in supporting sustainable land use and food security in the energy crisis that will determine our future.

As he was talking, I remembered that during discussions on the youth radio program 'The Art Room', a group of youngsters were heard defining creativity to their peers as "making use of what is around you to create useful or aesthetically pleasing things." I found their down-to-earth definition of creativity most refreshing. Whether painting, hand craft, or design, they emphatically said being creative involves using what is found around us and being aware of the environment within which we create.

According to this group of youngsters then, Mr. Guy is the ultimate cultural creative; his creativity provides working solutions appropriate to his surroundings and community.

The art students also described creativity as a 'universal force', implying that creativity belongs to everyone and is applicable to every area of life. Captain Guy has certainly demonstrated that, as creativity abounds in his successful efforts to grow and make almost everything he needs.

Just as there are exceptional elders amongst us, there are also youngsters who are an exception in their generation, developing a consciousness not dictated by consumer culture, but through finding out through study and experience, that things of real value and meaning lie within and around us, in the practice and exchange of skills and information. These youths may also be unusual in their willingness to embrace their cultural heritage, reinterpret it through a creative attitude and apply it to their daily life and future careers, rather than dismissing it as outdated and inappropriate.

So there is common ground on which the older and younger generation can relate, regrettably tenuous and not widespread, but it is something valuable on which to build. Wise ones are to be found in the old and the young, and it's my belief that a sustainable future lies in bringing these two together as a catalyst for productive action. The wise within any generation are those who think for themselves, create their own solutions and resist being swept along paths of waste and consumption that have no regard for consequence now or in the future. They educate themselves on environmental issues and realize that creating solutions to environmental problems through community action is critical to stop further degradation of the environment. Their knowledge and creations are not for them alone, but also to improve the life of others.

I give thanks to Mr. Guy for what he has taught me, and I look forward to learning much more from him, as we begin to build a bridge between the wise elders and the youth, who have the onerous responsibility of transforming depletive practices of their society into attitudes that embrace the art of resourcefulness as practiced by Lawrence Guy. He himself is cognizant of the urgency needed to build such a bridge and stands ready to help in its construction. Our elder counsels who know well the practical art of resourcefulness are not superfluous to society, they are our Belonging to landscape and heritage. A living fact that Micky Kirkwood would readily confirm, having his childhood roots more deeply grounded through the living interaction with Captain Guy of Top Village, Vermont.

Mr. Guy is a national hero in the here and now: living proof that a creative, youthful attitude is the basis of a long active life and a healthily grounded nation.

October 2007

Message from the Bountiful Moon

The power within the people who cultivate their bodies and minds with a forgiving culture through nature is far greater than those whose words fill corridors of talk packaged with the best intentions.

For the humble know how their words, thoughts and deeds are survival that creates stories, and laughter and Belonging.

10.

Free Spirit Moon

October

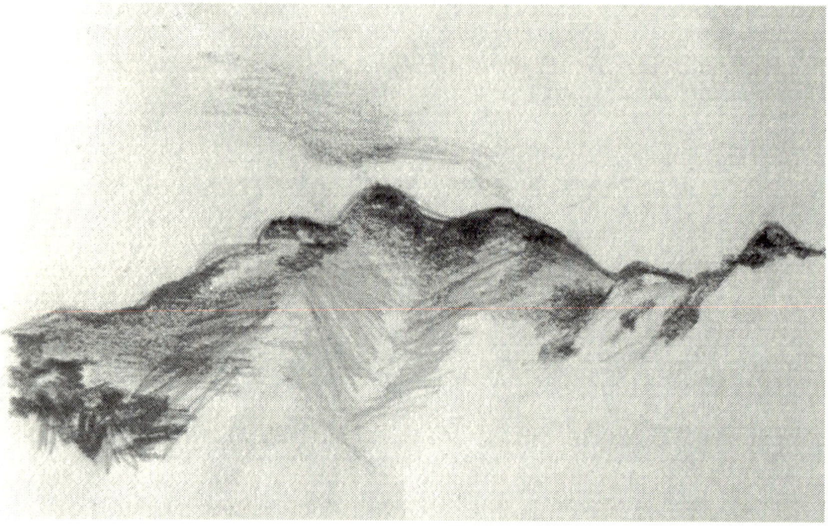

Within the mountain ridges are the valleys and the sky.
So peacefully she sleeps brimming softness

The Nature of Belonging

The Homecoming

The unique history of the Caribbean region and that of our own island villages is the story of migration. The majority of our population originated in far off lands; births taking place on these islands are an outcome of enforced migration. Our people travel to and from continents and between islands now as they have in centuries past. Those who don't relocate or travel overseas invariably have relatives who have migrated, retaining economic and cultural links with those in the islands.

Migration also takes place psychologically through human experiences in alien territories that define and redefine relationship with the homeland. Whilst often seen in economic terms, psychological effects of migration on intangible culture significantly affect this relationship through intercultural experiences accumulated by our students, diplomats, returnees, migratory workers in agriculture, nurses, recruits in the armed forces and employees on cruise ships. Migratory movement blurs the boundaries of nationhood, creates synthesis and relationships that can enrich us, and can confuse or clarify national culture and identity. It seems to me, that artists and creative thinkers especially, must be engaged in exciting journey of questioning our social and cultural origins to translate and articulate the effects of migration on our culture for our fellow citizens.

One of these critical questions, if we are to understand ourselves as a contemporary Caribbean community is, 'What is the accumulated effect of this history of migration on our present day lives and attitudes?' I shall attempt to answer this question simply from observation: it has created a great variety of peoples and mixture of cultures, of possibilities and expectations. We embrace new cultures readily and have presented the reality of cultural diversity as the central characteristic of Caribbean experience.

Migration has created prominent new cultural references that place altered expectations on the vernacular through inciting a craze for newness.

By comparison, the dearth of validated home-grown realities does not entice our youth who scan elsewhere for authentic experience. Looking beyond to other cultures for meaningful identity has also created differentiation and segregation among our people. Migration has simultaneously spawned added layers of existence that, on home ground, in a cultural climate of distrust (set down by divisive colonialism and picked up by partisan politics) intensifies suspicion of anything new and different. It appears that diversity has reinforced fragmentation. Acute senses of alienation and desperation to belong, to gain approval, coexist within our psyche whether on the islands or in the outreaches of the Diaspora. We are not comfortable with ourselves. In all our travels we have not found home, our belonging.

We make a very good job of ensuring those who feel they are comfortably home, wherever that may be, do not remain so for long. Divisions are acted out between herds of the affluent/middle class/poor; men/women; formally educated/unlettered; politicians and the people; the Afro/Euro/Indo descendants; even the artists and craft people are divided. Each group perceives the other with suspicion and distrust.

Caribbean people have erected hurdles of attitude strategically placed within the boundaries of childhoods to define modes of existence without which they feel society will fall apart. A privileged few are strategically fortified to surmount the hurdles. These leapers are apt to raise the hurdle higher for those that would follow. The system of segregation is thus self-maintaining and the camps are entrenched in minds more definitively than they are in visible locations. Where the boundaries are temporarily leveled between the social classes, closer inspection reveals that a substitute- party political affiliation- is firmly in place. The herding of minds effectively conditions the complicit to perceive themselves as different from other groups. In a desperate desire to gain entry a more prestigious confine, many people will perform whatever the vacuous selection criteria dictate.

Introduce into this an alternative possibility of being and its immediate rejection is predictable. The creative, inclusive attitude that dismantles hurdles of division, finds no place in containment, and so is cast aside completely. Dismissed as woolly and elusive, the creative attitude, unshackled by herding, is exiled from the prison cells and moves as a free spirit in a land where belonging is possible. Rejecting mental confinement, the outcasts turn their gaze away from human infighting towards the beauty of their homeland, the relationships that exist there and endless possibilities of love and connection. They see a land where diversity enriches experience, where everyone is one family, where healing the damage of centuries of separatism is possible. They see a land and people that need saving from self-imposed destruction.

The idea that we can be all things; proud of our African Ancestry *and* embrace Euro-centricity; be part of a group *and* appreciate what another group is doing; be an artist and also appreciate the craft person as an artist working with different materials, is an inclusive practical attitude which would put our history of migration to good use, creating a stronger cultural experience on home ground. The debilitating social effects of alienating the majority who set their sights on escape, only to experience further alienation can be transformed into fulfillment at home.

As simple as this seems, the transition from an exclusive perspective to an inclusive one needs guidance and education. Just as to 'love thy neighbour' is far easier said than done, thinking inclusively is also the result of constant guidance, self-discipline, and practice. The practice must start by cultivating compassion through a genuine appreciation for diversity as positive and interesting, not threatening.

Unless we are seeking power through domination, acknowledgment and validation different points of view and the different experiences of others, is not a compromise of 'self'. This simple difference in communication qualifies our sense of whether we feel belonging or alienation. The choice is ours-we create our own identity in how we choose to proceed: whether we unquestioningly accept to be herded into spiritual confinement or whether we choose to question what is put before us, to find out for ourselves and in the process become ourselves as the foundation of a functioning democracy. As Paolo Friere, Brazilian democratic educator said, 'The more people become themselves, the better the democracy."[28]

To simply 'be oneself' however, we know is not so straightforward. We have experienced aspects of socialization contrary to the 'becoming' approach to life.

In the context of our history of migration, the constant questioning of whether to stay or go, the yearning to leave for distant places and the resignation of those who have no opportunity to leave, is not only about physical relocation. Uprooted-ness takes place on a mental level, and affects our perception of our surroundings. Whether we stay or leave, these thoughts wrench us from our environment and rob us of a sense of collective belonging to our own communities.

The story of the Caribbean is one of movement of peoples to and from other lands, settling, moving on to other islands and returning. Africa is very much part of our migratory story, as is Europe. Caribbean people for decades have been preoccupied with the question, "what forms our true sense of identity and how has it evolved?"

We have apparently not found the answer, for there is endless searching and yearning. How can we turn the experience of being present to a positive one of belonging? How can we convince our youth that they are where they are needed and their contribution

The Nature of Belonging

is welcomed? This is the challenge of the teachers, the politicians, the parents, of every citizen who has a moral conscience. To nurture a sense of belonging within our youth, means examining our own thoughts and behaviour, embracing our own culture, respecting and preserving our own environment, becoming ourselves, so that our children may find peace and know that they are already home.

June 2007

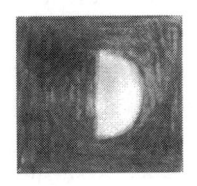

In Dependence

During the October, the month of St. Vincent and the Grenadines' Independence celebrations, I ask my students at community college what Independence means to them, and they usually tell me, "It's a holiday, Miss." Like most youngsters the significance of Independence is lost on them. The majority of our population was born after Independence and does not share the connection with the older generation regarding events of 1979. For the latter, Independence holds great significance: freedom through statehood and the end of colonization.

The importance of anniversaries of such historical landmarks in the Caribbean region is understandable when we consider that our ancestors were brought here against their will by a colonial power and thrown into these islands. Seen against this context, Independence gains significance as a gigantic step to reclaiming personhood.

Ravi Dev of Guyana, in his address to the CARIFESTA symposia forum in 1992 said:

> "All Caribbean people, by and large, are immigrant people. Our ancestors were brought here to fulfil a mission destined by a colonial power. The institutions set up by those powers, the structures they created, the forms through which we had to pass, the maze in which we had to survive, served their purpose, not ours."

The Nature of Belonging

If statehood means continuing to operate with the same mechanisms as those of the colonial powers, as suggested by Dev and many other eminent Caribbean critical thinkers, then what kind of independence we are celebrating?

The legacy of the colonies has continued in the administrative structures, where governance is prescribed by the subordination of one group by another. In the islands, this domination is enforced largely through partisan politics, which in southern island territories, is equated with ethnic groups. In other more racially homogenous states, domination is also based on social status through acquired wealth and education. Each of these divisive systems has its roots in the hierarchical power structures of the British Empire. It's a great tragedy that in the process of seeking acceptance through conforming to these systems, not only do we dismiss those essential parts of culture that developed outside colonialism, but that local customs are frowned upon. Although some aspects of it have been preserved as entertainment, local culture is generally thought of as a throwback to a past, which has nothing to do with daily life. This is one reason why the youth of today do not relate to it. As Barbadian poet, Edward Kamau Brathwaite, states, "We are spectators to our own culture."[29]

Cultural practices that developed independently from the colonial influence come from rural communities and are the only aspects of island life that can be hailed as truly independent. Daily practices that we take for granted-evolving as they did outside he colonial system-such as the Creole language, are tremendous resources of cultural information that developed independently of any school teaching. The people of the earth created new words through astute observation, transformed language into rhythm, gesture and content that goes far beyond words on a page. Spoken mostly among the rural poor, this language is gradually being schooled out of communities through the use of Standard English, which should comfortably co-exist with the local language.

(To grasp the cultural atrocity being performed, imagine a Spanish child at an English school who speaks her native language at home and with other Spanish friends, being forced to stop speaking her first language on the grounds that it's an inferior language.)

Whilst travelling in Cuba, I noticed many similarities between Vincentian Creole and Cuban Spanish, pointing to common African roots in expression. There has been little analysis done of this special language, yet there within its idiosyncrasies, its direct and intuitive expression, lies the essence of the Vincentian psyche. We often hear it referred to as 'bad English' thereby denigrating the creative expression and emotional intelligence of a whole people. The overriding message to our impressionable youth is that they must subordinate their own experience of being, to acting out 'better' imported cultures.

We are thus effective enforcers of modern day cultural colonialism.

The various Caribbean languages are just one example of local cultural practices that have developed independently of colonial influences. Many others are found in the villages as humble daily life customs that we take for granted. But rather than valuing them, rural people aspire to the values of the 'middle' classes, who in turn aspire to the values of another (British or North American) culture. Far from being independent, we find ourselves very much in mental, cultural and economic dependence.

Some Caribbean writers and artists have long been articulating the destruction of self-reliant local island culture, trying to define its forms, to build a vibrant Caribbean aesthetic in the absence of much needed institutional support. The arts have proven to be the most effective ways of reaching the youth and communicate the true meaning of independence to them.

One of the Caribbean's foremost creative intellects, the late vice chancellor of the University of the West Indies, Rex Nettleford, stated in his fascinating lecture in Kingstown (October 2008),

" Independence with a lower case 'i' is essential to independence with a capital 'I'. Creative thinking is an indicator of independence with a lower case 'i', but neglect of creative education has resulted in the inculcation of dependent thinking in our youth. This neglect persists in the bureaucracy of the region despite the fact that anything of value in the Caribbean has come about through exercising the creative imagination."

Despite their being marginalized as hobbies, Nettleford noted that poetry, music, dance, visual arts and sports have " through particular individuals lead to rich legacies for the region", their creations emerging as triumphant banners of a collective identity of a culture that's rich and unique. In realizing Independence, we must behold authentic culture, and examine truthfully what has sprung from those productive relationships of the people with their language, their landscape, gardens, handcrafts, traditional agricultural practices, natural healing practices. We must acknowledge that the sound of music on a home made tin or goatskin drum is the echo of our survival. And be proud of that humble and brilliant legacy rather than "presiding over its extinction" as Nettleford expressed our cultural demise.

The stigmatized cultural forms are in fact symbols of freedom being lost in the tide of commercialism and cultures alien to our spirit. Interestingly, but not surprisingly, these are the same forms that captivate our visitors from cultures that have forsaken personal qualities for systematic production for far longer than ours. Their hearts yearn, as ours do, for authentic experience. The struggle for Independence can be regenerated through creative learning that strengthens links between education and community and should be supported by festivals that reinforce a true understanding of the vernacular expression.

I suggest we start by initiating yearly community festivals, reinforcing appreciation for Independence through the vernacular arts: A Festival of the People's Language, a Rainforest Festival, a Festival for Natural Farming and Building, a Moon

Festival, a festival for boat building festival, or even one for hair-plaiting.

When the cornerstones of survival of an immigrant nation's dialect and other culturally creative practices are recognized as the epitome of cultural excellence, and when the institutions serve to actively promote that recognition, then we will have truly reached independence from colonization and lay rightful claim to a Caribbean civilization.

October 2005/ November 2008

The Nature of Belonging

Social Cohesion or Generational Suffering?

Upon being given a group multi media interactive task recently, one Community College art student wrote:

> "If you want to go fast, go alone
> If you want to go far, go together."

This statement written with conviction by a 17-year-old, shows wisdom and maturity far beyond what many of the older generation possess. It is profound in its recognition that working together is more meaningful and productive than competing with each other. It is also profound because this young person has seen beneath the conditioning that her young life so far has been bombarded with- the conditioning we all know that dictates we should live for our own self-gratification and personal ambition. Her statement was recorded on our whiteboard in the art room, along with equally profound statements from other college students:

> "NATURE should be your greatest inspiration."

> "To do Art is to see the world in a whole new way."

> "The world is what you make it."

> "Art is The Eye opener to reality."

"Humanity means human nature
Human nature is what we are
What we are is what makes us human."

"Just because you're misunderstood doesn't make you an artist- proactive thinking does."

"Always question EVERYTHING."

"All things are connected."

"We are all creative beings NOT human beings."

"What we do as artists is important to everyday life."

"People are afraid of what they don't understand."

"Look at things for what they really are and not what others want you to think."

"Do not let negative forces to alter your perspective."

Each one of these statements emerging from individuals within a small group of students bears deep contemplation. To truly appreciate their significance, we should first understand where they came from. They did not emerge from any book, but from the students themselves; they did not happen in isolation, but in an atmosphere of cooperation where students created a group installation that incorporated images, objects and words. It was, in their own words, " A story of what happens in the art room:

> a visual representation of what we learn and what happens."

The Nature of Belonging

Their collaboration was highly instructive, and they realized that it started with action, not with a plan or one authoritarian person dictating instructions to the others.

One remarked, " It was fun. I enjoyed it and it brought out a lot of things -it brought out how much we are together." The sense of togetherness was tangible, there for all to see in the form of a visual installation, a succinct and accessible documentation of the ability of our youngsters to think profoundly and to act together, with appreciation for each other.

The implications of this reality on society are as profound as the statements themselves. It seems that the consciousness the students express is exactly what the society needs to effectively move forward through seemingly insurmountable social challenges. And yet, as young people they feel tangibly oppressed, unable to act in accordance with their convictions. This is most puzzling as everything they express is in keeping with President Obama's philosophy of life and governance, that as a society we welcomed wholeheartedly, at least verbally. Some even celebrated openly in our streets after his being elected to office. Mysteriously, when our own young visionaries appear, we dismiss them with equal force that we welcome Obama. As one student said, "We are not taken seriously- the older generation thinks that we are much too young to have any input. We need more people to see what can come out of us." They also recognize that they are wiser than many of their elders:

> "We have gone through more than previous generation in terms of biological evolution. Our generation learns much quicker than previous generations. Three- year-olds are using computers. We inherit collective wisdom and mental quickness."

Evidence of this is empirically observed and recorded in the study of natural living systems and underscores the importance of consulting with and including the visions of the youth in social development. As one student clearly said, "We are not different- it's all about acceptance. We want to share and do and make our contribution to our communities."

This leaves, for me, one major postulation –apart from singling out a select few, how much are we doing to help our youths to fulfil their passion and birthright, which is to contribute to their communities in meaningful ways? How long will they be battling with lack of confidence, negative perspectives and self-images? How long will we relegate these youths to the frustration and ardour of rung-climbing a ladder of social pretension?

When I looked at the collective effort and statements of this group of youngsters, who consider themselves no different than others, (only in that being art students they feel woefully put aside as 'crazy'- a term I encourage them to reinterpret as 'independent thinker') I thought how these sentiments, put into collective practical action could heal the nation from a malaise of disenchantment with itself. I was once again inspired by the capabilities of our young people, but at the same time racked with sadness that these bright lights of social consciousness have to battle against being trapped by the pressure to clip the wings of their visionary spirits in favour of dull dependency on a society that not simply misunderstands, but harbours prejudice and defiance against them.

If all those in contact with our youngsters were to contemplate the possibilities of change implied in their optimistic proclamations, we could dismantle the crimpling assumptions that hold them back from sprinting vigorously towards their visions of possibility.

February 2009

The Nature of Belonging

Sister Pat, Moving Spirit

In every community there are people who bear testimony to the strength of the human spirit. They act selflessly, inspire and motivate others and ask for nothing in return. Such a person was Sister Patricia Douglas who lost her life on 20th May 2005 in a traffic accident in Barbados.

Sister Pat, Principal of St. Joseph's Convent Secondary School in Marriaqua, St. Vincent, was dedicated to the under privileged, and sought to enable them to uplift themselves through providing them with love, shelter and education. She knew that the ultimate price we could pay to God is to make the most of our potential, to develop our talents and to excel in whatever way we can on this earth. Deeply religious she was, but she insisted that a measure of her students' servitude to God was not the number of hours spent in church, but the time spent in disciplined study hours, learning and developing their God- given talents, working on group projects and community service.

The energy that fuelled her untiring devotion to a cause came from her spiritual strength.

She was a creative thinker, a problem solver, a doer. She would joyfully announce to her beloved Chemistry students at the end of class 'problem solved, matter fixed."

Her delight was in providing solutions to problems that would enable children to strive and achieve their potential. Quite often, people who have a vision work alone and are isolated in communities, finding it difficult to motivate others who become dependent on them and drain their energy. But Sister Pat had a gift of bringing people together in supportive networks to work on a common goal, like the staff at St. Joseph's Convent, the group of parents who built the school basketball court, and the Denniston Thomas Foundation, who are continuing with renewed dedication, the work she started for giving refuge to abused and needy children. The fact that the work she started will be continued with even more dedication, is testimony to the enthusiasm and motivation that she inspired in others. She was a truly a Moving Spirit.

Do we know any other moving spirits that are operating in our communities? It is time to take a look around and we will recognize individuals who are working quietly behind the scenes, for these people do not seek credit or recognition. Moving spirits are in all walks of life- and dedicate themselves to furthering the development of others. Their compassion enables them to feel as others feel and inspires them to act accordingly.

Quite often they are ordinary people seeking no accolades, or direct financial compensation for their efforts. They could be teachers who extend themselves beyond the call of duty; mothers who selflessly put their children's needs above their own; people who volunteer their spare time to a charity or community organization; the government worker persevering to get results within the bureaucratic systems that frustrate them. What distinguishes a moving spirit is that they do, they don't just talk. They are the people who recognize that things have reached a point where something has to be done and if they don't get together and do it now it will be too late. They are the ones that make the first move. Moving spirits are in turn sustained by the changes they see in people they got moving in the first place.

Sister Pat was an eminent moving spirit in the Marriaqua community. There are undoubtedly others in Vincentian communities trying to work with others to achieve their selfless vision. In identifying these people in our midst we should gravitate towards them and become moving spirits ourselves and start by

The Nature of Belonging

focusing on what we can do to assist others, particularly the youth, to develop their God-given strengths.

Tony Gibson, British author of 'Power in our Hands', who I was fortunate to assist in St. Vincent with some community projects in 1993, coined the term 'moving spirit' as it refers to a community member. He told me that after a long life of working with communities in Jamaica and inner city areas initiating self-help schemes, he noticed that real change and development comes from ordinary people working as moving spirits.

He said:

> "Some politicians and academics see ordinary people as voters and taxpayers who have to be coaxed or intimidated into handing over power and money so that others can do the job. It turns out that they can't do the job properly on their own any longer. But here and there in the world, ordinary people have found ways to take a hand in doing what needs to be done and when that happens, things change. At first in very small ways, eventually on a mega scale. It's happened in the past, It is happening now."

Sister Pat excelled in doing what needed to be done and making things happen. Her response to challenge is expressed in her own words that she loved to repeat, "Problem solved. Matter fixed." Under her guidance and enthusiasm many problems were solved in and out of the classroom, and many matters continue to be fixed by those she inspired with her love and enthusiasm for life.

A fitting tribute to her would be for all those who were privileged to have known her to recognize their own ability to be free, moving spirits and create change through making things happen in our own communities.

May 2005

Message from the Free Spirit Moon

Compassion and mental freedom are partners and requisites for meaningful change. They belong to the cause of suffering

Those who work freely with compassion in their hearts will be missed when they are gone but gloriously remembered, not in minds. They are ever present, for the same spirit with which they toiled is moving through those whose lives they touched. And Beyond.

11.

Forest River Moon

November

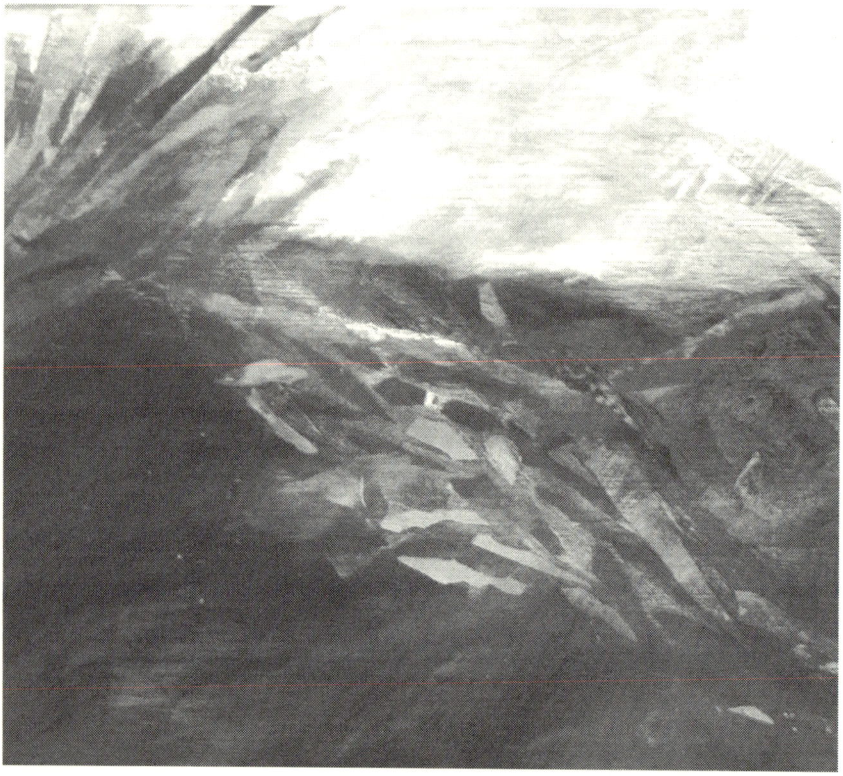

The river called me back and I listened to its bubbling voice.

"You are water flowing, each obstacle slightly changing your course, but not your eventual destination. Your fragments will meet again to join in the composition of life."

Homeless Island

Whilst many Vincentians were swept up in the pre-election political feting of November 2005, a few gathered one Saturday night at the Peace Memorial Hall where a book launch took place of a collection of poems written by Vincentian poet and musician Ellsworth "Shake" Keane. The book was entitled 'The Angel Horn', after Shake's last poem written shortly before his death in 1997 on his way to Norway. Although I arrived in St Vincent ten years after Shake left for New York in 1981, I became familiar with his work and life through Edgar 'Doc' Adams' collection of local writers' publications and by talking to people who knew him.

The book launch featured a recording of Shake reading one of his poems- an unforgettable experience for me as I had never heard his voice before. Vincentian poet Philip Nanton, presented Shake's story through a brilliant interpretation of his poetry.

Shake's wife, Dr. Margaret Bynoe, gave a moving account of the sequence of events that lead up to the publishing of Angel Horn. Well-recognized and celebrated as a jazz musician in Europe and New York, Shake's creative vision born of his Vincentian roots, is his legacy not only to St. Vincent and the Grenadines, but globally, as his work resonates a truthfulness that befits all great art works throughout history.

The audience was reminded of many critical issues that evening through the various reminiscences and recitations. The greatness of Shake's poetry that brilliantly captures, often in Creole dialect, everyday things in new ways – entices us to reinterpret what we

The Nature of Belonging

take for granted, and look at ourselves in depth and sometimes with humour. But his concerted efforts to uplift the cultural development of his country were defiantly thwarted. Within the labyrinth of government offices, he was incapacitated by repressive attitudes and subsequently by his own grief.

We were reminded of the struggle of the committed artist, of how the surrender of inner conviction befits a small island's colonized society. Shake's wife stated that he was deeply saddened by his painful experience in St. Vincent; it affected his life to the extent that he lived his last years mourning the loss of his country in cultural exile.

As Shake's book launch ceremony proceeded, and we heard from the speakers about different aspects of his story, the elation of sharing recognition of great literary works was, for me, mixed with an air of melancholy. Whenever I hear Shake Keane's story, my heart becomes heavy with sorrow for the anguish he suffered in a culture restricted by anti-creative attitudes. The pain he felt upon reluctantly leaving his beloved homeland never left him. The sorrow I felt lingered through the celebration and into the informal exchanges that took place afterwards. I attempted to qualify it further. Was it empathy for Shake's island mourning, or possibly sensing the expansive loss to his island? Was it identification with my own struggle for voices of creativity to be heard? Was it the fact that some speakers had remarked how disappointing the attendance of the event was considering the eminence of Shake's work?

In this, they should not have been surprised, as all artists know there are many distractions that prevent comprehension of living truth amidst a culture of consumerism and political wangling. Schooled in the proprieties of selling out, our population sniffs at the offerings of local poets who through earthy Creole, are driven by a desire to write to express the creative vision that lies dormant with in us all- a vision that has the power to connect communities and nations.

The sadness that lies within the heart of the Caribbean artist is grief and mourning for truthful expression that is dying, and in many peoples' lives, has never lived at all.

A sense of grief lingers, as the artist is reminded- and all those with whom the works resonate -by the minimal turnout at Shake book launch; we are reminded day after day that our systems of social organization reject what is society's liberation and identity- the gift of creative expression.

Shake's work expresses the authentic unadulterated culture of the people. Pure art, like the jazz music that he loved, is not always easy to understand, not always comfortable to hear, sometimes challenging but always true. His plight is shared by the few non-commercial artists in our society, for not only do they tell the truth, they reinterpret the mundane, the ordinary, they challenge the way the establishment conditions and controls society. These artists are creators of the unadulterated and the adulterated world will always ravage the artist, as it ravages all that is authentic and natural.

Shake's poetry speaks of nature, of landscape, of folk culture, of love. Today's mainstream island society values none of these things, for nature is pushed aside, landscape polluted, culture is imported, and love is swamped beneath lust, violence, power and wealth. So no wonder Shake's story is melancholy, for in his work and life we face the truth that rises above the insincerity and pretence of daily reality for most. If Shake were alive today, as the plight of the authentic artist becomes more challenging yet equally vital, one wonders would he ever have been able to return to live in the St. Vincent that is rapidly commercializing beyond recognition and whose politics drives a deepening wedge between its people. He articulates the sense of being an outcast and society's obsession with an artificial culture in one of the last poems in his book, 'The Islands (A Toast)', where he writes,

> "St. Vincent proud, diminished, giggling, homeless island, cannot protect, digest, cannot interpret its own."

Not a day goes by when Shake Keane, the man I never met, leaves my side, for his words capture the reality of my daily life. And that night I reflected on how the launch of his book passed almost unnoticed against the backdrop of political electioneering, symbolizing the debilitating, consistent, plundering of these diminished islands of their artistic genius.

November 2005

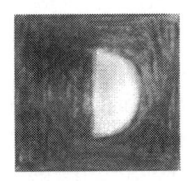

A Nation of Designers

The word 'design' can be used to refer to the appearance of something, but especially appearance as it relates to use or function. Designing is the process of putting something together for a specific purpose. So we talk of something as being well-designed if it functions well, and badly designed if it does not. The act of designing involves developing an idea through to a finished product or service. Successful design takes many things into consideration, and creates balance between variable elements within set limitations. It is an analytical, complex process, involving comprehension of mathematics and proportion, materials, uses of tools and technology. Design is thus effective problem solving that employs multi-dimensional thinking to ensure a product, or outcome, is entirely appropriate. Something that has been well-designed will automatically have aesthetic quality, sometimes referred to as 'style'.

Design fields studied at university degree level include architecture, graphic design, industrial design, automotive design, interior design, landscape design, fashion and textiles, video arts, animation, sequential art and many more.

Although design is a study discipline in its own right, the basics can be introduced into primary education from projects that develop critical thinking skills in young children, to more complex projects for secondary school students that require research and analysis. Design projects can teach mathematics, social sciences, history- in fact all subject areas as they embrace arts and science. Art, design and science are all founded on in-

The Nature of Belonging

depth observation, recording, research, making discoveries and conclusions. It is a limited comprehension of these subjects that creates a perception of them as separate.

Nowadays, in St. Vincent and the Grenadines, with no structured creative studies in our school curricula, and the visual arts/art and design subjects marginalized as 'art and craft', our present concept of design is not developed. When making or building something, we often overlook the design process altogether, resulting in things that are poorly designed.

And yet, traditionally, without formal education, Vincentians were excellent designers. They were experts at identifying a need then thinking out ideas before creating a solution for every day life that functioned well from what little was available. Our predecessors were highly creative problem solvers. They understood the qualities and characteristics of different materials and how to use them effectively in various situations. Children, too, skilfully designed toys, customized carts and vehicles from recycled materials. They were engineers in no small measure. Design knowledge was accumulated over generations and handed down from one to the next ensuring that even the simplest objects were suitable for their purpose whether toys, baskets, hats, tools, furniture or even the traditional house. Traditional boats are examples of outstanding design where different styles were designed for different purposes- the Bequia whaleboat, fishing boats, and the Carib canoe.

A characteristic beauty radiated from these humble objects for daily life, an aesthetic that is at once visual and tactile, one that asks to be taken up and held in our hands, one that desires contact and relationship. It is accessible. By studying the design skills of our predecessors we can learn a lot about designing for today and the future. Unfortunately learning from tradition is no longer valued; rigid education systems and consumer culture have turned us into copyists. We consequently embrace forms that have not developed within, and are not appropriate to, our environment. As a result we are confronted with many objects and buildings that do not function well.

The Kingstown Central Market, known as the "Vegetable Market" is one such example, designed by a European architect who apparently did not research Caribbean small island culture and economy of the people for whom the building was destined to occupy their daily lives. A fundamental component of all great art and design, is independent enquiry through research (finding out), the sourcing of visual, oral or written information.

In the instance of the market, interviews with the people who have to use the building, would have been pertinent to its eventual design. Their livelihoods may have been enhanced by a building design appropriate to purpose.

As it is, much encased wasted space blocks the views of surrounding mountains, having swallowed up the town's tiny central park, where people used to meet informally. The building is devoid of Caribbean character, and fails to draw people inside, so that the businesses on upper levels cannot benefit from a flow of pedestrian traffic. The vast amount of concrete and steel used in its construction no doubt benefited those who supplied the materials, but has rendered the building poorly ventilated with little natural light. Fundamental to its poor design is a total lack of understanding of Caribbean market culture, which had the architect been aware of, he could have created a building in keeping with the needs of the local people, rather than imposing those of an individual architect on a community market culture.

It is a tragedy that a desire to improve the daily lives of people is no longer a criteria for successful architecture. In this case, a misplaced design agenda resulted in hard working people suffering losses in income and having to adopt a desperate sales manner as each vendor hustles and competes for precious little business. Many still trade out on the street to survive, so the market failed in its original purpose, which was to clear the streets of vendors, and has created ongoing confrontations between the Town Board officials and market vendors.

The Nature of Belonging

The market building is one of many examples of local design that do not suit the society's cultural or economic context and as a result negatively impact the people's quality of life. Poorly designed structures can cause great inconvenience and suffering; just as appropriate design can greatly enhance and improve daily life. Harmoniously designed work environments and living spaces impact positively on state of mind and productivity of workers. We can imagine the attraction of a well-designed market space where people are assured of regular passers-by, where the atmosphere is conducive to browsing and spending time, where spaces are incorporated for people to congregate, play musical instruments, display visual arts and handcraft, where natural light and plants can create atmosphere.

Imagine the same space utilizing overhead space efficiently, so that displays can captivate visitors to spend time and money. A small park or leisure area could have been included in the complex. A practical alternative could have been erected for much less cost as a large open space under a sturdy roof, supported by Kingstown's characteristic city arches. Instead, cold rectangles of mirror glass behind iron bars confront us as we pass through our town centre.

Design, then, can be assessed by how well an object caters to purpose and its surroundings, through a practical use of space, and/or a process of planning. Design awareness is the ability to discern appropriateness to function, which ordinary Vincentians once demonstrated in designing their homes, according to their needs, personalizing their space. Design impacts on all structures, objects and planning, including town planning. Everything we can see that is wo/man made has been designed, for better or for worse. Good design basically begs the question – is it practical? If the designers do not ask this question and proceed instead to design according to our personal tastes and preferences, then we are imposing a great injustice on our fellow Vincentians' daily lives. Once something so common as to be utterly taken for granted, we seem to have abandoned design awareness as we adopt structures, systems and products designed for other environments. Starting with an understanding of the people and their culture, with active participation of their communities, we can address human needs through appropriate design.

Our predecessors relied on their expert design skills for their survival in the past. Our present lack of design awareness from the highest levels of the society down, compromises our survival and quality of life, creating a reality of inconvenience and compromise that the vendors in the vegetable market know only too well in their daily struggle to survive. As a consequence, our children do not know their history of exceptional design, nor do they know that they are exceptional designers.

March 2005

The Nature of Belonging

Fresh Growth: A natural development

The price of modern development is easily observed to be underdevelopment of nature's domain, evident through the impoverishment of rich soil; the cutting short of healthy tree life; the massacre of nature's intricate community stripped of its right to peacefully co-exist. Like the elimination of the First People that belonged to her, nature's ways have been systematically banished from the lives of those immersed in consumer culture, industrialization and modern development.

Widespread destruction of green life is effected through the complete ignorance of hardship that awaits the 'civilized' initiator of the massacre, complicit in his own undoing. Psychological disturbances and neuroses are early symptoms in these beings of a much more devastating price to be paid for damaging the planet's immune system that has created a potentially fatal disorder of climate change. Initial signs of an impaired nature consciousness may go undetected by the 'civilized'. The removal of the sole surviving patch of greenery in Kingstown city, preceded years earlier by the extraction of a regal avenue of eucalyptus trees from the approach to the city, were early symptoms of our impending disconnect from nature. The desertification of coastal areas, creeping inland with environmentally irresponsible building and development, are more advanced stages of the chronic condition, caused by depriving life-giving forms the right to exist.

The lack of compassion towards nature is no sooner demonstrated than it is extended into human relations. The disconnect that began selectively contained, seeps further and further in through total self-absorption of the civilized life. And though we may assume that rural communities are resistant to the deadly scourge, symptoms are evident there through drastically reduced plant diversity. Only a decade ago, it was customary to exchange plants and herbs with neighbours in rural communities, but with the lure of (mostly toxic) alternatives that line supermarket shelves and freezers, the range of edible plants in our gardens and farmers markets has dwindled. And yet, in the tradition of natural healing, we have everything we need to address our local depletion of life force through immediate action of replanting our communities. Such a measure would begin the recovery process, reviving consciousness to undertake the next stage of implementing reforestation programs, renewable energy systems, ecological architecture, land regeneration and water conservation projects.

So if we have remedies to rehabilitate our green resource, why do we hesitate to deploy them? Is it that our rapacious addictions have become all that we know? Do we think it's uncivilized to cure through cultivation? We have literally cut nature out of ourselves. Admiring her beauty in photographs and brochures does not transmit or preserve her energy. She is not a pretty picture, not at all. The generation that hacked her to pieces and then views her composition intact in sentimental images, have no solutions for her recovery. The violation and nostalgic admiration demonstrate extremes of disconnect from her essentiality of being. Both belie the perfected detachment of the mercenary. What we practice on nature extends into our social relations- we cut down our living sisters and brothers and glorify them in words and pictures after they are gone.

The preservation of our environment and human life itself now depends on care and concern through a proactive attitude of the youth towards natural resource management and the lifestyles they choose. Therefore they must be the pioneers changing the flesh and blood attitude by forging paths of spiritual recovery through loving connection with nature's kingdom. As the environmental

The Nature of Belonging

age has dawned in distant places, our youths are opening their senses to the excitement and possibilities of fresh life, among them a minority group of students who work on art and ecology projects. They study the complexity and beauty in nature through using drawing not as illustration, but as an investigative tool leading to discoveries that have transformed the way they see their environment. They recognize the wealth of information stored in natural forms and patterns, and how that information can be used to create powerful and effective designs of all kinds, from architecture to textile design; patterns of self-organization that apply to agricultural systems and even provide lessons in community building. They notice that compared to the beauty of the natural world, the man-made world is badly designed and does not function well.

But the most powerful lesson for them is that preservation of the natural environment is fundamental to our survival and we must act immediately to protect and regenerate it.

Through their creative studies and visits to our elder farmers, they are getting to know what nature has to teach us, so that we can instinctively understand what needs to be done—and what must not be done—to work in harmony with its processes. So inspired by this realization are they that they intend to use their creativity to enlighten others on matters of grave concern, by organizing presentations to student groups, and through a weekly national radio program[30]. These youngsters realize that creative artist/designers can no longer stay detached and preoccupied with their own self-image. Social and environmental problems are so acute that that creative energies must be channelled productively into socially responsible action. With the dawn of the global environmental age, action based on caring for every living thing will replace the tearing down that has engulfed our progress. These youngsters must be commended for their mission, reflecting a shift of awareness from destructive self-absorption to an exceptional vision of service to society.

As nature itself welcomes new growth and makes room for it in the natural order, we must welcome transformative actions of the youth, and allow them to fulfil their course for present and future generations. By isolating and marginalizing them we are going against natural processes and the social order practiced by First Peoples' cultures that left us the legacy of an unspoilt environment.

It is obvious that those weaned on industrial age values have perpetrated environmental destruction. It is time to construct enabling conditions where creative thinking of the youth can follow its natural course. Let us not wait until our islands look like a death land product of the industrialized north, where nature is preserved in sentimental images. A life-threatening emergency calls for urgent attention to healing and recovery.

As protest songwriter Bob Dylan sang over forty years ago as the environmental age dawned:

> "Your old road is rapidly ag'in'. Please get out of the new road if you can't lend your hand for the times they are a-changin."

April 2006

The Nature of Belonging

Soil Searching

Like the biological workings within our bodies, many things we cannot see sustain life, not least of all the soil beneath our feet. The soil has a delicately balanced complex anatomy of its own, evolved over millennia according to its precise geographical location.

Unfortunately, healthy soil can now only be found in places where nature is undisturbed by man. But careful observation of such a treasure heaving with life reveals many secrets for the passionate farmer/gardener. They would initially observe that the forested earth from which vibrant trees and plants flourish is covered by fallen leaves and beneath them lie others in various stages of decay. Having not been trodden or pulled around, these layers are comfortably aerated. In their moist darkness worms, insect species and micro-organisms copiously populate the layers of dead organic matter, eating and excreting to break down into nutrients that feed the plants. A diversity of plants collect and store various nutrients such as nitrogen, phosphorous and potash. Tree roots hold the layers of living populations in place and animals in their natural habitat recycle organic waste and fertilize them. This ecological system is self-organized and its survival depends on the entire composition of working parts. It can be understood as a total living organism comprising many parts from tiny single cell creatures to larger, visible forms. The pristine soil is a living sponge storing water for continual nourishment.

Now introduce modern man to the living soil, whose predecessors lived harmoniously within this system. He cuts the trees, clears the nutrient-rich plants, digs and turns over the soil, exposing it to sun and rain. Initially the nutrients contained in the soil after centuries of caretaking by the ecosystems, feed his crops (from the fertile soil that we are blessed with) but after several harvests the land is not so productive. The system has been overturned and sabotaged.

The modern land worker notices that where once birds came to feed on worms exposed by man's handiwork, the fields and banks are now bare. The soil has changed colour from dark rich brown to light red, clayish and sandy, missing its organic component. It is no longer breathing moisture but is dry and thin. Gone are the insects and micro-organisms that cannot survive in such harsh conditions. Into the lifeless soil he now introduces petro-chemical fertilizers that artificially boost the growth of seedlings and plants, and fuels dependence on artificial means to mimic a natural process. Like the addict searching for happiness deluding himself with artificially induced euphoria detrimental to his health, we similarly inject chemicals into our soil-stream to get quick results, at the expense of a healthy soil, and healthy bodies that consume its produce.

Many farmers in our village communities know this scenario well. Most of them remember times when their crops flourished without the chemicals and people were healthier without artificially forced foods. But not many remember how to farm without artificial inputs and have become dependent on them. They regard a natural alternative as too much hard work, but there is no one working hard in the forest to maintain the system. They have simply ceased to observe nature's self-organizing systems in action.

Destructive farming practices have dug us deeper into ignorance and we have buried ourselves in misinformation. We must protect the fertile land that's left in its natural state and regenerate depleted lands through sustainable farming methods. No digging, no artificial inputs, no burning. We can plant our manures: fast growing trees, plants and grasses provide feed for animals, and green fertilizers. Debris, clippings and cuttings should not be burned but used as organic material to cover the soil. Water running off the land presently wasted can be harvested through contours and terracing. Nature will get to work once assisted in this way and redress the balance for us. Once the requisite elements are in place, she will invite her workforce of industrious creatures to help rebuild our blessed fertile land.

A healthy agricultural soil and healthy people are interdependent. As our bodies heave with the weight of over consumption and ingested poisons, our hearts falter with the overload of toxic thoughts and we perpetuate a life-threatening culture. Nature generally, and the soil particularly, bemoan their neglect through our inability to observe and connect the loss of soil quality with our own health and social problems.

We can begin to heal ourselves and our environment with nature's help, but first we must respectfully acknowledge the existence of a self-organizing, life-sustaining organ beneath our feet.

September 2009

Message from the Forest River Moon

In the flowing river all things are possible
Our reflection in her is tenuous
but forest-river remains
millennia steadfast.

But then, an interference
in the last second
of their existence
diminished rivers cry thirst
as human charges uproot their source.

Great gifted humans, like water,
also diminish in our presence,
cut out of their living community purpose
to be managed in glorified artifices
that line walls and corridors.

But the powerful river
calls back its precious charges
and unifies those who
move like river, think like water.

The source is replenished
by itself.

12.

Returning Moon

December

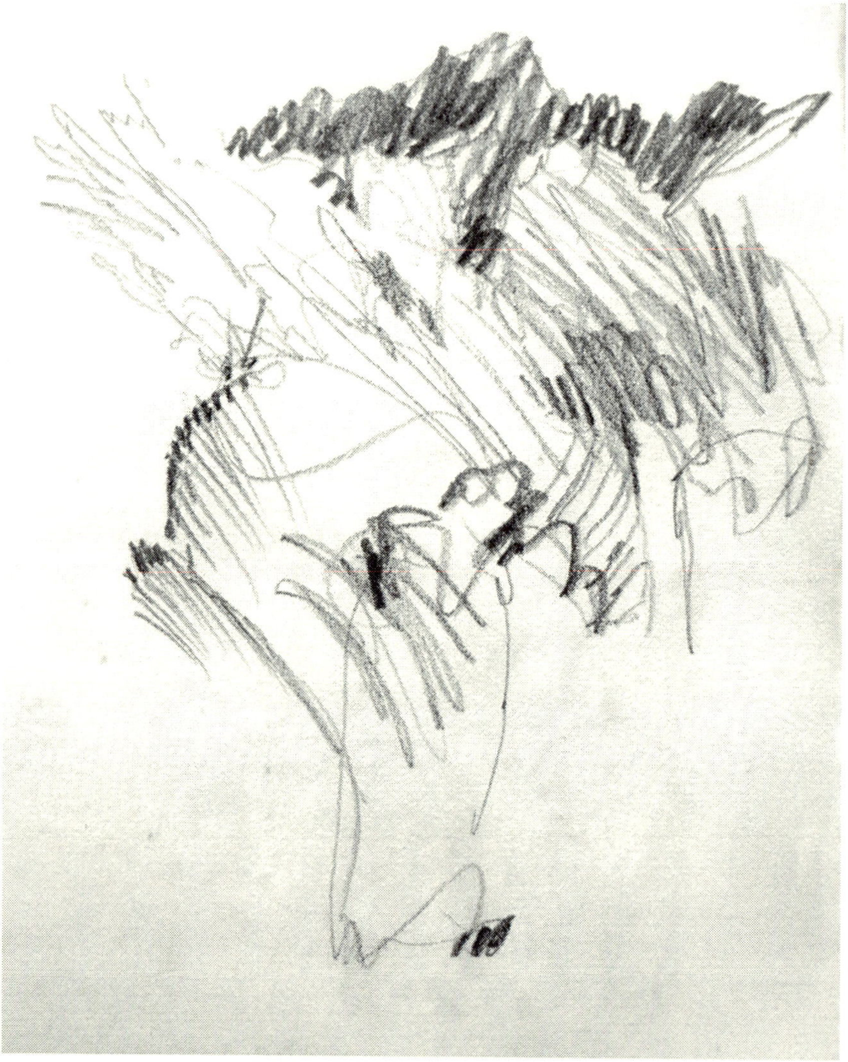

Mystical landscape disappearing, reappearing;

"reality is in the interludes," the mountain tells me.

Our Caribbean Sister
1. Culture as Experience

Architect of Old Havana's restoration project, Eusabio Leal, stated in the closing of the cultural development conference that I attended there in June 2007, "culture is what remains in us when we forget what we have read in books". In other words, culture is **experience** and culture is what I have experienced in Cuba- culture as art, and of course, as music, performance and dance, but culture also as exchange between people and the environment, experienced as the expression of actual feelings.

This intangible culture of feelings and relationship is one that we seldom acknowledge, let alone preserve or focus on its quality. But in my opinion, ignorance of the importance of intangible culture is the root of spiritual poverty that manifest as social problems that we know only too well. There are many possible perceptions of a country and life itself, but essentially direct experience is what forms our reality. For instance, many may talk about positive aspects of economic development in a country in terms of figures and percentages, but if we can't walk the streets safely at night, those figures may not mean anything positive in terms of our own experience. We may also be convinced that having a large house and domestic staff is pleasing and desirable, but if we are paranoid about being robbed, those pleasures of affluence become a hazardous liability, which is the reality of affluence. The sensory and emotional feelings of intangible culture, eventually determine the quality of our existence. And these feelings are based on our interaction with our immediate environment.

Interestingly, in Cuba there is no fear of being molested or attacked, the streets are safe and there are no traffic jams. In Cuba, parrots can be heard squawking in residential areas because trees are planted everywhere. Nature is highly visible, organic farms extend between main roads, a city dweller can purchase organic produce from a corner shop, and power cables run between the branches of trees without any threat of the tree being severed from its roots. Nature is not dominated and sacrificed but actively nurtured to play a major role in life's experience. The proliferation of nature is recognized as an important aspect of ensuring the security of future generations.

Cuba is a country where the verges on the highways are landscaped with flowering trees, a place where so much is produced, with seemingly little rush because of the cooperation between people, the high degree of organization and mobilization of human resources. Sexism is non-existent in the workplace, reflected by the high number of women professors, and government officials. Unlike in some English-speaking Caribbean (small) islands, women can express themselves without evoking ridicule or jealousy. The Cuban revolution, it seems to me, was really the replacement of an attitude of domination and exploitation with the attitude that everyone is equally valuable to society and must all work hard for and with each other. An attitude focused on life as quality, fulfilling experiences as opposed to material accumulation. Now, this attitude may be labelled as dangerous, communist and terrorist, but the reality is in the experience, which in Cuba is actually peace, safety, aesthetic beauty both in nature and design and the spontaneity of the people.

So if you, enjoy eating healthily, devour the arts and crave intellectual stimulation, if architecture fascinates as history preserved in buildings that reflect an ultimate respect for the ancestors, if music with content and complex rhythms, imagery that expresses rich imaginations; if those things are what you treasure, then Cuba will be experienced as a total overhaul-an enrichment of mind, body and soul.

If, on the other hand, you are more concerned with one-upmanship, adulation through wearing the latest fashion, cell phone gadgets, cable TV and so on, then you will find Cuba somewhat limiting. It will not provide the arena that many seek where power and influence equate with money. From that spiritually compromised perspective, the experiences of the soul will pass you by in Cuba and elsewhere. Those people who refuse to visit Cuba and complain about her, reflect their own inability to open up to experience – a common outcome of conditioning of a materialistic society that compromises the imagination and thus the ability to respond to the forces in creative action and the elements of nature. It may be discomforting for many who have succumbed to the propaganda to hear that life in Cuba can be experienced as expressive yet peaceful, culturally vibrant and safe.

This account of my personal experience may be very disturbing to those inculcated with the politics of domination that primes us to be consumers at the expense of our mental and physical safety. But therein lies the contradiction of what we have been told and what we experience for ourselves. There is much to learn from Cuban culture if we could think of experience as a critical part of learning instead of passing judgement without it. The experience of those at the centre of Cuban resistance is reflected in the words of Abel Prieto, the Cuban minister of Culture, "culture can be an antidote against consumerism and against that many times repeated idea that only when one buys can one feel fully developed and happy in this world. It's about planning culture as a way for personal growth and self-realization –it has to do with the *quality* of life."

In other words culture is quality of **experience** and that is, speaking from my own experience, exactly what Cuba has to offer.

July 2007

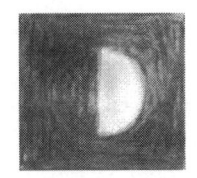

II. Wellness Below the Surface

Different types of agriculture, the majority organic, are practiced all over Cuba. In the suburbs of Havana organic urban agriculture is common. Through force of necessity, derelict pieces of land between buildings have been turned over to food production. Each urban farm has its own sales outlet, so that communities can buy fresh produce within walking distance from their homes. Creative solutions have been used to develop organic fertilisers, harvesting worms (lombriculture), companion planting and composting.

In Cuba there is no shame in working the land, farmers are among the highest earners and the field attracts engineers, artists, doctors and scientists who bring to the practice a good deal of analytical problem solving through innovative integrated systems of mixed farming. But even more interesting than methods and technology, is the manner in which the systems are put into practice in cooperative groups, where observations are shared, and everyone makes a contribution to the planning process. Paralleling the model of sustainable ecosystems, these groups recognize the individual as indispensable to the whole. Community spirit and cooperation is the most important factor in the ability of Cubans to rise above every challenge that faces them from revolution to embargo, food security, to catastrophic hurricane damage.

Many of our Caribbean students who study in Cuba seek security in the company of other foreign students and miss the most important lessons to be learned about her community fabric. Other visitors to Cuba focus on obvious structures and infrastructures, art forms overlooking the intangible elements indispensable to the production of great accomplishments in any field. In many ways, Cuba has preserved what we have lost, and we merely skim the surface of lessons that lie within her shores. Gaining technical expertise in Cuba is good, but without an environment of practical collaboration, this knowledge will not benefit our communities (as the under utilization of graduates from Cuba upon their return proves.)

In the twenty or so years since Cuba has been educating significant numbers of our islands' citizenry, have we stopped to consider how Cubans cannot conceive of education without creativity and culture? Cuban students are confident, expressive and have a thirst for knowledge about other cultures. It is generally understood there that cultural education unites the people psychologically and spiritually and engenders cooperation.

Rex Nettleford warned us at his 2008 Independence lecture in Kingstown: "we must move from individualism and opposition to collective participation- a fact that we ignore at our peril." He went on to say that instead of continuing "the apprenticeship in sabotage," we must develop our concept of education to embrace "a life-long reality of fellowship" which our present neglect of cultural education opposes. "We could take hold of the legacy of spirit of independence," he said, "the resourcefulness, coordinated social action bequeathed by our fore-parents who worked the land. Their energies that were once exploited can be utilized." He reminded us, "by continually degrading our Earth-based legacy, and practicing opposition as the modus operandi in our daily lives, we are perilously averting meaningful progress."

From our own observation and experience, as well as that of eminent creative thinkers, it's evident that cultural education leads to a sense of identity/belonging that in turn fosters participation and communication; stronger communities; environmental awareness; food security; more productivity (including a better tourism product); less crime. In other words, our social and economic security hinges upon our ability to relate harmoniously to each other. I would humbly add that it also results in happier people (although tragically, happiness never surfaces on negotiating tables, confused as it is with endless consumerism).

Sustainable agriculture that feeds Cubans through alternative methods, ultimately depends on community relations that are built on cultural education. A nation that can feed itself understands what lies below the surface, and digs deeper within its own culture to unearth the most important lessons for a sustainable future.

November 2008

A Crime to be Happy

On an early morning trip to Kingstown recently, I encountered the usual morning traffic, the lines of cars crawling through Back Street, and police directing with their characteristically serious faces and authoritarian manner. I eventually reached the Grenadines' wharf for my daughter to embark the ferry to Bequia. Entry entailed proceeding through large gates, manned by various layers of serious-looking security personnel. I found myself wondering how this beautiful morning in St. Vincent was so solemn an experience for us all -as yet in our travels I hadn't seen a single person smiling. As the security guard at the third gate checked the dollar port fee and boat ticket, I asked him, "And how are you this morning, sir?" He forlornly said he was trying to make himself "OK"; the poor man was already visibly stressed and this was just the beginning of the day.

I drove back through the town past more serious faces hustling to work and briefly stopped to buy fresh ginger at a supermarket. At the vegetable counter, I asked myself , "How on earth could ginger have reached $8 per lb?" I was jolted back into the reality of the cost of living rising dramatically in the last few years. Not much reason to smile there. Could this be why people have lost their jovial countenance on the street and don't smile or laugh- because most of us are stressing over to how to make ends meet?

The interlude at the supermarket was to delay my return journey ideally as, with perfect synchronicity, I drove out onto the road behind a large truck, full of prisoners on their way to conduct a day's labour. Suddenly, the atmosphere of the morning changed, from the sombre stressed-out looks of people in town and the obvious presence of police and security, to a truck of about thirty animated prisoners filling my vision without a warden in sight. And what a jubilant crowd it was- here I saw the first smiles of the day, through the exchange of jokes and laughter in the early morning sun; Vincy humour on display like a Carnival J'ouvert band through the street. The prisoners captivated the attention of passersby and the exchanges of 'yeah tanty' and 'nuff respec' and 'tell him I go organize' lit up the faces of the public, some in their porches, some sitting by the roadside. All were visibly happy to see the prisoners pass as they left a stream of waving spectators. This sight restored my faith that the jubilant Vincy spirit is alive and well, as I remember it in daily life years ago.

My return journey home was enjoyable and memorable thanks to this band of faded denim warriors on a mission. They looked around them at every detail in the landscape, breathing the fresh air and savouring the dramatic sea views. These men were visibly enjoying their island like visitors to their own shores. As their laughter rang out with their calls to the public, positive energy spread in their wake flooding the winding road.

Unlike the people going to work in town, the captives were facing a hard day's work with positive attitude. They were connecting with everyone they passed, enjoying and appreciating their surroundings. Living in the present moment.

I abruptly reminded myself that this is part of the population who are incarcerated and wondered if being in prison is a source of happiness (we know the stories about criminals who commit crimes to go back in jail), or do the adverse conditions in prison make them appreciate what's on the outside? The most significant question I asked myself was, "*why* do they appear so much happier than everyone else out on the street and are able to uplift others with their good cheer?" Their employed peers, hustling to work, as owners of vehicles and property with access to hire purchase, appeared positively stressed and miserable compared with the prisoners on the truck. Those on the 'inside' seemed happier and carefree, spontaneously appreciating the simple pleasures of life, like fresh air, a simple exchange with others and the landscape.

Possibly experience has taught the prisoners something that many of us do not know, that happiness is not about a chase for bigger and better things, but about each present moment, our sensations of sight, breath and laughter; about feeling positive in miserable circumstances. Is this our lesson from the prisoners, who some may label as a bunch of wayward offenders-a lesson as important as the key to happiness? How ironic that, deprived of their freedom, they should be the minority who demonstrate the spontaneous Vincy spirit that was once a daily reality in our communities. Could this be why some re-offenders beg to be sent back to jail? Admittedly there must be some very unpleasant aspects to incarceration, but are these outweighed by camaraderie and freedom from rising prices and financial struggles?

The robust sight of the denim posse on board a truck may well be an endangered aspect of our intangible heritage, as the prisoners will soon be relocated and sightings may well be far less frequent. What, or who, will take their place to uplift the spirits of people in the street? The increasingly prominent billboards and advertising that greet us there, do not put smiles on the faces of 'free people', they compel us to spend, and separate us into political or social camps. The sighting of the prisoners, on the other hand, held a far more unifying, positive attitude framed in connective experience of our surroundings and of eachother.

It seems we have much to learn from subcultures found in unlikely places, the few remaining footholds of our intangible heritage, but we may not appreciate them until they are gone- or will we be too stressed to even notice?

April 2009

Returning Moon

Happy Cash Returns!

The original function of community festival celebrations was to consolidate community values and provide a diversion from the rigours of daily life. In St. Vincent and the Grenadines, our traditional festivals of Nine Mornings and Vincy Carnival in December and July, bring together local islanders, visitors, and returnees from overseas. An added dimension has developed as increasing commercialization shifts our festivals foci from forging stronger community ties to individuals' spending power and business sponsorship. Corporate sponsors and the private sector use the occasions to aggressively market their products. Yearly holidays have become opportunities to entice people to purchase.

A trip into town at Christmas time provides ample evidence of this: street vendors proliferate, desperately competing with larger businesses, customs offices are heaving with frustrated people, car parks overflowing. Banks have interminable lines of customers. Stress levels rise dramatically as we attempt to increase our purchasing power for the rapidly expanding market. But who is really benefiting from this frenzy of commercial activity? Most of the goods we race to purchase are imported: hams and turkeys, clothes, furniture and household accessories, alcohol, tree lights, the latest electronic gadgets. The working person finds what little disposable income they possess is accounted for before it's earned. What was once a festival of joy and release from worries of daily life has become an intensely stressful experience. But apparently, this is a sign of economic progress.

People without disposable income can have their spending power boosted by access to special Christmas bank loans promoted through the media. At the annual carolling contest, a bank choir could be heard heralding financial loans. This puzzled me so much I have to ask endless questions which will no doubt, equally puzzle those who see economic progress reflected in impulsive spending. But my questions are:

Is there a moral conflict in utilizing carolling contests to promote bank loans in the season of 'unconditional' good will, as such loans are not benevolent, but designed to make money for the lender? The same poor person who may have difficulty getting a loan to set up a small enterprise encounters few constraints in being saddled with a Christmas loan. Is this not encouraging poor financial management? Will such a lending scheme not create further domestic hardship for households where children will go without some basic needs of food and clothing as parents struggle to repay loans that profit corporations? Do such schemes create further dependency and dig people even further into poverty? Is it possible to make profit without creating suffering in other people's lives? Are the principles of socially responsibility and corporate business practice irreconcilable?

The answers to these questions would not alter the fact that we are rearing a nation of shopaholics. The values from the industrialized world are upon us, consuming our minimal financial resources and peace of mind. Robert Dallek, John F. Kennedy's biographer wrote: "The humane government looking out for the powerless or less powerful is a necessary counter to business interests that think primarily about the bottom line." Do we have humane governments providing measures to counteract constant powerful advertising campaigns that convince us that we need their products to have a better way of life? 'Free' enterprise it may be, but it is desperately expensive for many.

Various studies on the psychology of human happiness have confirmed that once basic needs are met -shelter, food, clothing, education - quality of life experience depends on personal relationships and self-development based on communication skills and caregiving (not owning things). Of course our ideas of basic needs are changing- no longer are we satisfied with a modest house- we want bigger and grander houses, faster and more luxurious cars, the latest cell phone package deal. Enough is never enough.

But we can see for ourselves that a grandiose lifestyle does not usually lead to happiness. People with wealth often fearful of losing what they have become consumed in protecting it, and as targets of envy, alienate themselves from those who are outside their social clique, thus dividing communities into levels determined by individual ownership.

Within the context of long-term national development, consumer culture is unsustainable, it degrades the environment, and local enterprises cannot compete on price with mass produced imported items, leaving many poor people trapped with few lawful options for livelihood. The culture of consumerism has gone so far, it has even hijacked our festivals that were initiated long ago to simply bring joy to the community. It has tricked us to think that unless we spend lavishly, we cannot enjoy our own seasonal festivities.

The carolling promotion of bank loans was the ultimate display of economic imperialism, where people's cultural expressions are hijacked as a vehicle for profit-driven advertising. As another year ends and a new one dawns, reflection reveals that we are on a cycle of mental enslavement to an economic power. The socialization process ensures we remain in permanent competition with eachother and obstructs our unification.

The communities that created our festivals were certainly not materially well endowed, but yet the open-hearted communication they practiced, the storytelling and sharing, the legacies from communal living, catered far more effectively for fulfilling the emotional needs that our sophisticated modern-day surveys tell us are prerequisites for happiness.

The Nature of Belonging

This community life had a cohesive system of governance and deep spirituality, a powerful aesthetic tradition. But colonizers throughout the world labelled indigenous culture as 'primitive' and 'dangerous', and regarded it with suspicion. (What could be more suspect than a Christmas carol designed to exploit poor people?) The community values of love and compassion, of 'do unto others as you would have them do unto you' are ones that are desperately needed to rebuild our communities.

But how can these values survive cultural hijacking by an economic regime that trains us to do unto others what we would not want done unto us? How do we entice community members to begin the disciplined practice of compassion that requires no financial outlay?

A man who devised his own solution to this question is Dr. Maulana Karenga who in 1966 introduced an annual festival called Kwanzaa into the African American community. Modelled after the first ancient Egyptian fruit festivals, Dr. Karenga's vision was to promote restoration of community values among African peoples in the Diaspora. He was deeply troubled by the disintegration of community through obsessive self-seeking and violence.

Kwanzaa was initially practiced as an African-American celebration but is now observed by over 20 million people worldwide. The Afrikan Heritage Foundation of St. Vincent and the Grenadines led its first Kwanzaa celebration in Kingstown in December 2007. A family occasion, Kwanzaa starts on the 26th December until the 1st January and each day it focuses on one of seven principles:

Umoja- Unity in the family, community, nation

Kujichagulia- Self Determination, to define and speak for ourselves

Ujima - Collective work and responsibility, to build and maintain our communities

Ujamaa- Cooperative Economics, to build businesses and profit together.

Nia- Purpose, to make the collective vision of building community

Kuumba-Creativity, to appreciate and enhance the beauty of our surroundings

Imani- Belief with all our heart in the righteousness and victory of our struggle. [31]

These seven principles are founded on the practice of compassion, which lies at the core of every religion. They also are the basis of democratic and creative education. They are universally accepted as necessary practices for moral and cultural development. These are principles embraced by great leaders and all who have sought to uplift the human condition. Only the most mercenary would not agree that the practice of these principles is desperately needed in our societies. Certain institutions could benefit from a practical understanding of Ujamaa and discover, like Mr. Yunus' worldwide Grameen Bank (p. 14) that there are ways to empower the poor through socially responsible money-lending.

As these principles of empowerment and liberation were central to African community life, it is no wonder that imperial forces effectively deprived the enslaved of their culture leaving them spiritually impoverished. But are we now consciously choosing a seductive commercial package in place of similar imposition? At this time of year we thoroughly flush our homes and personal spaces of debris in the Christmas cleaning ritual. Let us similarly clear our minds through questioning the programming that pollutes our mental and cultural space.

Happy Kwanzaa to all our brothers and sisters, to our family in humanity. May we rebuild our community through the spirit of caring that created our festivals- born because we had relationships to celebrate, not because we had money to spend. Songs sung to liberate, not to delude. In peace and love, every day is the beginning of a new era, holding lasting possibilities for change if we dare to believe in ourselves, and be free at last.

December 2007

Message from the Returning Moon

Long ago life cycles revolved under the heavens punctuated with returning festivals of common unity celebration.

Modern people with packaged culture and modern stresses do not make communities. Community is found in unlikely places, among those removed from the onslaught of advertising and stripped of their paraphernalia.

What is to become of the unlawful ones who step closer to understanding happiness? How will their knowledge find a place in the open prison of finance? Will their voice be heard from the margins of modern distraction?

Once, not long ago, it was told in stories and heralded in song.

13.

Blue Moon

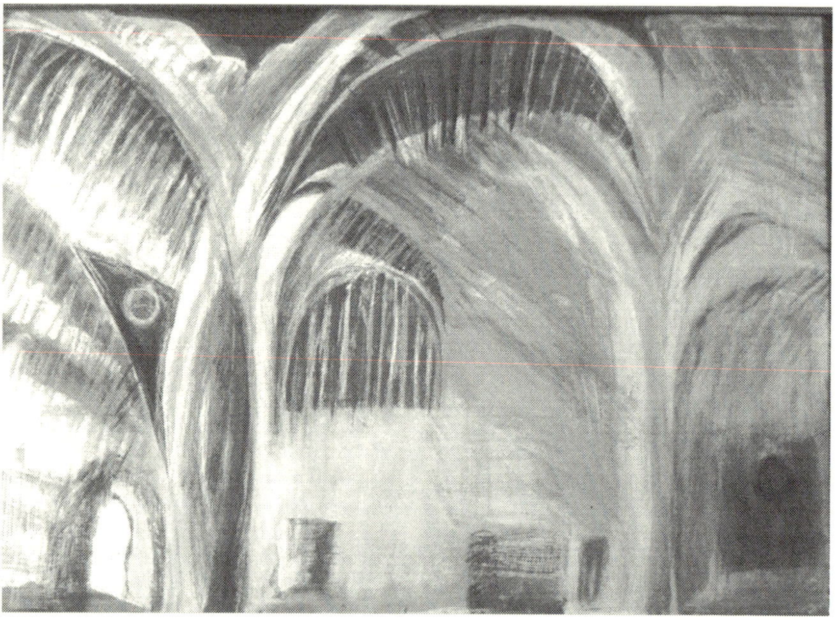

You are the silent light of love. You are blue peace.

"There are some places one should venture without another. The shadow (immortal) realm is created in absence."

Timeless Moon

It is common knowledge among rural people in tiny quarters of our little island, that the moon is a force continually influencing inhabitants of the earth. But this knowledge and how it evolved is of little use to those maximizing their personal interests on the rest of the island. As we encase ourselves physically and mentally, we have limited our capacity for depth of perception. But if we were to peek through the door of curiosity and tilt our heads skywards we would bear witness to a much more convincing reality......the timeless movements of planets in our mighty solar system.

If the earth is Mother, and sun is Father, then moon is Child, and her mystical phases the product of their timeless rhythmic relationship. The solar nuclear family are dynamically balanced, each with its own atmosphere, contrasting yet complementing each other. The mysterious cosmic beauty of the moonchild's metamorphosis from dark to brilliant is a miracle of synchronistic perfection.

The pure wonder this movement inspires in our gazing ignites the child in us, normally suppressed by fixed matters, entrenched in problems that a sense of wonder could heal.

The relationship between Earth, Sun and Moon is endlessly in motion, changing, shifting, yet always harmonious. The mystery of the solar system and its galaxy awestruck ancient civilizations who calculated lunar and solar calendars from their observations of celestial planetary alignments.

The Mayans, who occupied our neighbouring continent, developed the most accurate calendar in existence and had a precise understanding of our solar system's cycles, believing that these cycles coincided with our spiritual and collective consciousness.

Their acceptance that our lives are interwoven with the rhythms of floating planets, compelled by polar attraction and repulsion seems like a fantastic projection of the imagination to earthlings immersed in material preoccupations of modern-day life.

And yet, if you ask an island elder about the moon, they will tell you differently. Her phases, visible in the sky, are not merely a backdrop to busy human life, they are working their connection through every particle, every molecule of water. While her illustrious light enchants, the magnetic pull of the moon is not visible. We commonly accept her influence on the sea tide but simultaneously on inner subtle levels her rhythms wax and wane in unseen places.

Once, not so long ago, she brought island villagers out to bathe in her light by river or beach, to play ball games and tell stories in communities who lived with the moon as our neighbour. She has not left. She continues to shed her light ebb and flow upon our fitful lives. She is still there as bold in our presence as she was when our ancestors listened to her peeping eye. She shares with a marginalized majority the humiliating sense of being present but ignored. This, she muses wisely, is a painful transition and patiently awaits sensitivity to re-enter our consciousness to embrace our natural surroundings as part of our experience once again, like gifts from a welcome neighbour.

When they were young, our elders, who understood the force behind her beauty, planted and harvested by her phases and this knowledge was passed down through many generations. Community life in the islands was consciously connected to moon cycles, when farmers knew the rhythms of nature; they tuned their actions to them, much like a sailor navigating the wind and sea currents. They harvested bountifully in service to the elements. They knew that the moon affects the tides and the water table level, and thus the moisture in the earth and plants

The Nature of Belonging

and trees that are connected through water, and that energy flow through the moon's gravitational pull affects the movement of fluids within soil and plant tissue.

In the phases of increasing moonlight when sap flows more strongly, filling plants with energy and vitality, the planting and harvesting of crops that mature above the ground is favoured. In decreasing light it is known by moon gardeners and farmers that the energy is oriented towards the roots, making this a good time to plant and harvest root crops. Harvesting bamboo is favourable at this time, as the glucose levels in the woody fibres are decreased and less likely to be devoured by boring insects. The moon's gravitational effect on the flow of moisture in soil and plants, the effect of moonlight on seed germination, were all considerations of the traditional gardener. As two-thirds of the human body weight is water, it's highly likely that the moon affects our energy levels and emotions.

Traditionally, many religions recognized the importance of the moon phases. Ashangta yoga observes full and new moon days as holidays. Monthly worship of Buddhism is regulated by the moon four times a month; at full moon, new moon and the days in between. The Hindu calendar, like the Celtic one, is based on the lunar cycle and the movement of the moon, with the year divided into thirteen months. The Jewish Passover is celebrated on full moon and the following eight days.

The moon in all these religions is seen to be female, linked to the unconscious and a powerful force connected to the basic cyclical rhythms of life. She is healing and therapeutic. Based on their understanding of the solar system, many ancient sources describe time as being circular. Accordingly, the wisdom and powers of creation possessed in ancient times will come back to us again.

To live in the flow of the moon is to acknowledge our place in nature and that we are cradled by universal forces connecting us to the rest of humanity, past, present and future. Everything else within our control we may seek to change, but this ebb and flow of universal energy remains a constant, out of the reach of controlling hands.

To live a life oblivious to this primordial reality is surely to dislocate from the heartbeat of nature. Her kingdom revolves in accordance with laws, yet the presumption that mankind can thrive in ignorance of the natural order has prevailed throughout the industrial age.

So determined have we been to control and destroy nature, we have lead many thousands of cultures and species to extinction, endangered thousands more, and disrupted the cooling system of the earth, causing sea levels to rise. The ghastly folly is coming to light through glaring ecological imbalances in response to which a rapidly growing movement of conscious and creative people are embarking on projects that implement corrective practices. Such positive action takes place from a renewed compassionate perspective of the Mother Earth as sacred provider that embraces the interdependence of all upon, above and below her surface. From such a perspective, time is no longer about hustling money, but about timeless Spirit.

This alternative perspective is a parallel reality that can be felt through the great force of Belonging, as easy to reach as tilting our heads to look skywards at night. The vision of the patient moonchild invites us to take a deep breath, embrace her healing feminine power and sense the pulse of the universe that is ours.

September 2009

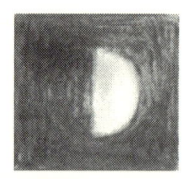

Test of Natural Intelligence

Most of life's lessons I have learned and continue to learn emerge from observing nature without preconception, or expectation, just quietly observing with an eye that has been exercised through engagement with visual arts, but began as the primary tool of childhood learning through exploration and discovery. The thinking eye of observation is our greatest teacher. Through watching, looking and listening and absorbing without barriers, one learns an enormous amount that has immediate implications on our daily life.

For example, working in my garden I observe every detail of growth, colour, surface texture and rhythm as one does in the practice of creative arts. This visual information leads into a world of discovery about balance and harmony and the relationships in nature's eco-systems, about health and vitality, death and decay. Such discoveries have much to teach us about our own relationships and place in the natural order of our communities. Nature has proven herself to be a thousand times more fascinating than the glossiest art gallery or museum, more extraordinary than anything wo/man could make or design.

Since I was a teenager, my observation was exercised through drawing practice, but now is constantly at work without effort or exertion. Practice renders any skill second nature, as learning to drive or ride a bicycle demonstrates. I work with students to develop their observational skills, not only for art and design work, but also for the most important lessons of life learned by observing ourselves and our environment. When our vision is opened up through practice, the world becomes a place full of excitement. We have a childlike sense of discovery. We are alive. A simple walk down the street is full of information, patterns, rhythms, movement, where every visual exchange has meaning. 'Free entertainment' I used to call it as a teenager, where at college Manchester, UK, I found much to observe and learn from even in a dismal, cold-grey city devoid of nature.

I discovered through drawing, observation and questioning, that the appearance of something, its surface texture is the result of structure and function of an organism. Beneath this surface lie complex structures, patterns and movement, interrelationships-a wondrous world of mystery and discovery. The mystery of life itself can be gleaned from these wonders that surround us if only we choose to observe. One simple example of life's lessons learned from observation is how, despite weeks of drought and no rainfall, a banana body (trunk) is full of water. Working in my banana field, I often stop to think about how incredible that simple fact really is. Human beings could not survive more than several days without water, but plants and trees have amazing coping mechanisms.

I am regularly stunned by the beauty of this simple fact-that all around the plant may be dry and harsh, potentially life-threatening conditions, but inside is full of water, wholesome and vibrant with life. The banana tree has not taken on the conditions that surround it, but preserved itself, intact. This natural ability has brought sustenance to human beings and their island economies. Upon closer examination of this incredible phenomenon, exhibited to some extent by all plant life, the ability to survive is held in the mystical workings of cell structures and the beautiful continuous patterns they form within the plant.

To extract further lessons from such encounters with nature we can apply these simple observations to ourselves as human beings. We are surrounded by an emotional desert of social tensions; destruction of life and healthy relationships through greed, violence, envy, addictions. Our peace and spiritual wellbeing is

The Nature of Belonging

threatened by as harsh a drought that threatens the survival of plants. And yet, unlike the banana plant, we seem unable to create within ourselves a dependable survival mechanism. Instead, our communities absorb what surrounds us and we become physically and mentally unbalanced. We dry out, parched and unable to respond and adapt healthily to adverse circumstances and, as if in a delirium of spiritual dehydration, we deplete what we need to preserve, and exacerbate the drought. Of course our children emulate this treacherous behaviour.

This is why I often wonder who is more intelligent- a plant or a human being? Nature could thrive without us, but we cannot survive without her.

Only a few hundred years ago aboriginal people on all continents lived off the land without any damaging effects to nature, and were all but eliminated by civilized and intelligent, educated people who set about creating global warming and climate change.

So I ask, what is intelligence? Is it demonstrated by destroying what you need to survive or is it being able to live in harmony with what, if observed and respected, can provide more than we need- lessons and knowledge, raw materials, food, medicine, textiles, buildings, functional items, water, energy, diverse living systems and Beauty, the inspiration of the creative imagination.

But for some of us this is not enough, we want an artificial life with purely man-made things around us. Nature can disappear, for all we care; an attitude that has brought about the imminent destruction of the planet.

Through observing natural living systems, where they remain, we can learn survival strategies from nature in these perilous times; strategies that are not self-limiting but create networks of interdependence. The simple act of observation can lead us back to the understanding of harmonious place in the natural order.

As I observe and work in my garden, I wonder about all of this, particularly why we choose spiritual evaporation over learning lessons that cost nothing, over opening our eyes to be instantly launched into a new beautiful space where the loving arms of nature are ever open, ready to provide sustainably and share her mysteries. Like spoiled children we reject what she can teach us.

So tell me again- who is more intelligent, Nature or us?

March 2007

The Culture Haven

In a rural corner of Penniston village, on the leeward side of Yurumein[32] Island, a blossoming of creative consciousness takes form in the growing and planting of trees, building with natural materials and making things for daily use from the gifts of nature that surround us. The activities are simple but profound. They tunnel into the host of resources before our eyes, through an innate inquisitiveness that fills our culture of being now, as it has for centuries.

The basic media of these forms of creation are the natural elements of earth, air, wind, sunlight and water, whose fluctuating dynamic gives life and form to plants, human beings and the myriad of phenomena that spring from their mystical interaction.

Hand2Earth, as the Penniston experience is named, actively constitutes a conscious recognition of the movement of these elements through time and space. It provides a place where their dynamic engulfs the human beings who align themselves to a co-creative process with nature. The amount learned depends on the innate sensitivity of these human assistants of nature, the more they are able to submit to nature's complex intelligence, the more of value will be learned.

One aspect of the purpose of such a venture is to help to raise, within the island's youth and others, the necessary sensitivity toward the natural environment upon which our collective survival depends. The elements of earth, air, water, sunlight, and the fibres that spring from them, form a delicate interplay; a dance of life that can draw us into the wonder of scientific and aesthetic experience. To experience such an engagement is intensely personal, and at the same time, encompasses group purpose. It can quite simply make us productive in empowering ways. Hand2Earth's purpose is also to heighten our perception (not only intellectual understanding) of our natural resources- the power in our hands and hearts, the earth and the grasses, trees and the rocks, the elixir of life, water- as they have been smothered by external distractions thrown over us like an impermeable blanket through which we cannot breathe our history or destiny.

In this suffocating darkness, cries for authenticity are muffled as apathy triumphs over effort. Our hearts and hands become limp and lack the vigour of contact with a cause. We live in a heavily blanketed sleep unable to respond to the prodding and pleading of wakefulness. Meanwhile, nature pines for her partners along the journey of a living aesthetic, her grief made deeper by the wrenching memory of past communities who recognized her daily as the mother of life. But she does not subside into oblivion with the weight of her grief. In every corner, in every blade of grass, anywhere that the interplay of elements creates form, she pushes through lovingly with messages for our ailing spirits.

Hand2Earth is a collection point for her messages. A cultural haven where they can be translated back from their forgotten past into active, productive communication through making things of intangible value such as healthy farming and healthy eating; harnessing the free gifs of nature and creating energy; working in partnership with nature to regenerate the soil for sustaining living systems that include human beings. It involves finding solutions to environmental challenges that threaten the life-force of the land and these solutions are specific to the history and geography of the location. It involves creativity of the highest order.

Hand2Earth may be the first such project to take place in the Emerald Valley watershed, but it has much in common with many environmental justice initiatives taking place globally. It proceeds hand-in-hand with its sister project in the valley, lead by Vermont resident Laurence Guy, an elder who is lovingly investing

The Nature of Belonging

his lifetime of experience in his community by demonstrating the organic propagation and processing of indigenous tubers, fruits, and spices. Such initiatives are the outcome of nature's persistent reaching out to her human partners. The makers and doers with playful, energetic spirits will be most receptive to her calling. For they will understand through a childlike wonder, the enormity of her influence as far-reaching into future generations of children.

As we fill our senses with the messages from nature, they will come in all forms- through the sight of her colours and patterns and interplay of relationships that inspire artists, designers and farmers, crafters, engineers, to the sounds she generates through the elements of wind and life that captivate the musicians, the poets, that unify and give direction to the hunted; to the textures we feel against our physical and mental membranes, textures that integrate structure and vibration, weaving them into a protective shelter that cradles our being. But above all, her gift is one of a wholesome spirit, an inner peace that grows in direct proportion to time spent interacting meaningfully with natural resources that are around us.

Our interaction with her can start and continue by simply looking and listening with no intermediary; by breathing the sweet breeze with relish and appreciation; by noticing the elegance of a water droplet in its descent from leaf to ground; by standing beneath any tree of choice and looking skywards, becoming the connection between roots and branches; and by learning important life lessons from the reverence with which the earth receives water, then lovingly utilizes it in partnership with sunlight to nourish and produce.

(In many places on our island's earth has been sadly robbed of this spiritual right where, due to our interference, rainwater washes away the earth away instead of being absorbed by it.)

These exquisite experiences are freely accessible to all in the true spirit of nature.

Such simple contemplative practice can begin to heal and correct the imbalances within our relationships, the devastation heaped upon our natural resources, and provide an experiential basis for action towards the betterment of our communities.

It's a natural choice. Partners in Hand2Earth have made that choice silently, knowingly responding to their island calling that reverberates from mountain to sea. A calling that echoes with the silent intentions of all those who yearn to belong to themselves, a silent longing to breathe freely through their natural senses and at last come to rest in a haven deservingly created from the most meaningful interaction; love in action through nature.

July 2009

If you are interested in learning more or working with partners at Hand2Earth, visit naturalbelonger.wordpress.com

Natural Steps to Belonging: Practical Action Sequences for Self-Discovery and Community Healing.

Appropriate solutions to global social and economic crises are being seen all over the world to come from direct observation of our surroundings, a collaborative partnership with nature and compliance with:

> NATURE'S LAW: We must put in to take out, without force.

The observant eye notices that non-compliance with this fundamental law of nature spells disaster and amounts to arrogance of domination demonstrated by humans more than any other species on earth. Imposed systems create more harm than healing.

Although action can take many forms at different levels of organization, here are some simple suggestions to align us with nature's law and help to rebalance her living systems, which include human communities.

Action Sequence 1

Aim: to rebuild the soil (earth soul), purify the air, and ensure clean water supply:

Step 1: Carefully select and plant a tree then notice how it feels.

Step 2: Plant more trees
Step 3: Plant a tree with someone else
Step 4: Plant trees with someone else in your community
Step 5: Plant trees with your community

Action Sequence 2

Aim: To emulate Nature's no-garbage policy to reduce national waste output; regenerate the soil (soul) through increasing worm population, contribute to local food security.

1. Collect all your waste paper, newspapers, cardboard and fabric scraps (biodegradables only) in a separate bin from other garbage.
2. Place it over your garden lawn in beds shaped to your own design. You can dig narrow pathways in between beds first placing removed soil to raise up the beds.
3. Cover paper waste layer with grass clippings or chopped leaves. (a technique called 'mulching')
4. Allow worms to proliferate and do their work (approx six weeks), then plant a variety of seedlings in beds by simply making a hole through the mulch.
5. Replenish mulch regularly from your steady supply of paper waste and organic matter- cut leaves, grass etc.
6. Observe what happens to the soil over time compared to the rest of your lawn.
7. Keep a notebook of your observations and discoveries.
8. Continue to observe, plant, harvest and discover.

Tips:
-Spread animal dung before spreading initial paper mulch layer.

The Nature of Belonging

-Control pests by mixed planting, herbs and marigolds and using natural pesticide e.g. diluted hot pepper spray.

Remember you are rebuilding your soil after years of neglect, so be patient and thorough. Observe which plants do well, focus on the process rather than the produce. Eventually as you co-create with nature, your yield will proliferate.

Action Sequence 3

Aim: To further reduce housekeeping bills; reduce chemical soil pollutants; protect your skin and washing machine; recycle wastewater in the garden.

1. Place 1/8 bar of blue (carbolic) soap or waste fragments of same soap into a squeezy bottle full of water. Allow it to dissolve into a thick liquid.
2. Use as a substitute for washing dishes and laundry detergents.
3. Redirect the safe wastewater to irrigate the garden.

(This action will also support the small island economy of Dominica where 'Bomber' Clothes Soap has been traditionally manufactured in 3 colours)

Action Sequence 4

Aim: Improve mental and physical health; reduce stress; join the growing global environmental movement comprising environmental activists; ecpsychologists; natural farmers and builders; deep ecologists; creative educators; down-to-earthers; ordinary people!

1. Follow Action Sequences above.
2. Experience a sense of Wellbeing.

3. Go and show someone else how to do it.

Practical tips for rejuvenating the disposition and community life:

1. Think of nature as part of your community, and your community as part of nature.
2. Start a seed and seedling exchange in your community
3. Start a recycling project in your neighbourhood primary school. It will eventually spread through the community.
4. Involve children in these activities.
5. Laugh a lot
6. Listen a lot.
7. Observe nature a lot.
8. Reduce time spent watching others, (but increase time watching if they are doing any of the above!)
9. Network with local and regional grass roots organizations and projects.
10. Give thanks daily for the sumptuous life at our fingertips.

Message from the Blue Moon

Do as the moon does, emerge from the shadow again and again in resplendence of Belonging!
   Onwards into the New Moon of Resolution..........

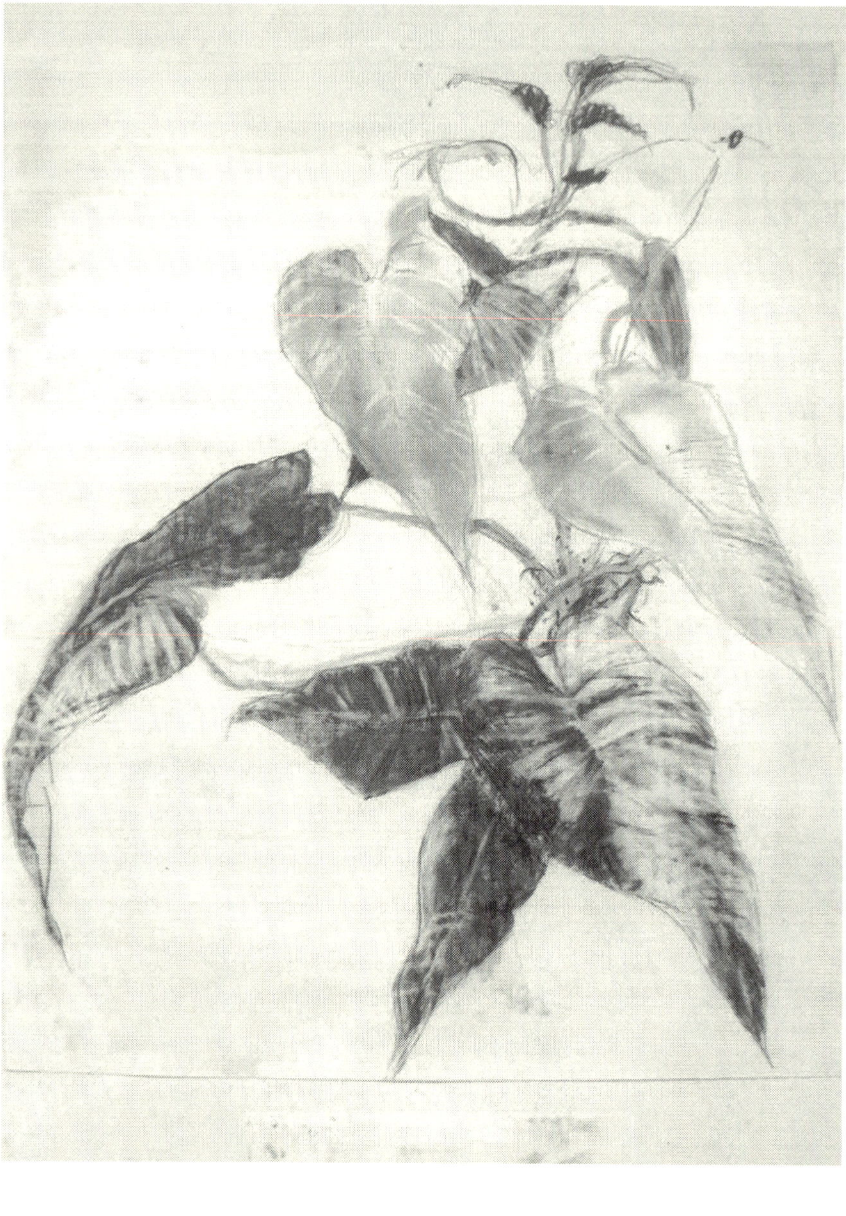

Afterword

A Life of Nature Ramblings

An Interview with Vonnie Roudette by Gillian Goddard for Green Thumb Magazine, October 2008

Q: How have you moved forward successfully in a challenging environment?

VR: I think a simple answer to the question of how I have moved forward (if indeed I have!) in a challenging environment has to be answered as having a dialogue with nature that gives me spiritual strength and guidance- a connection that was built on the foundation of a childhood in Africa where I had direct unlimited access to nature and village life. Ever since, I have sought Her out, She is ever present within me - even through years of city life as a student in UK and Japan, where I studied and lived for three years in a rustic mountain dwelling on the outskirts of Kyoto.

So even when humans present us with the toughest challenges- as we are wont to do- the divinity in Nature has guided and given me strength. In this way I have been able to withstand and navigate many 'setbacks' that have eventually served to qualify my purpose, which is revealed to me through those actions that She (Nature) guides.

The dialogue with nature was given expression through my 'imaginings' as a child and later explored through my art and design work which for many years was the source of my income in Europe through painting, textile design, theatre design and lecturing.

I returned to the Caribbean where my family roots are (Trinidad and Dominica) eighteen years ago, specifically to enable my children to have an experience of community life in nature. We lived in Trinidad before the mountains of St Vincent beckoned us and drew us into their bellies in the Buccament valley. And here I started to garden and wander in the fields and mountains. I knew my career as a designer would be impossible to pursue from here, and noticing the need for creative education I was beckoned by a desire to help others on their creative journeys.

I set up weekend classes for children and evening art classes for adults. I struggled financially for three years, taking on freelance work including some video production jobs. Two crafters, Nzimbu Browne and Margaret Roache and I founded SVG Create in 1996, an organization for artists and craft producers, then an opportunity came as Handcraft Development Consultant for the O.A.S. between 1996-2000, when I worked with craft producers all over the country focusing on design development and marketing. In 1997, I set up Fibreworks Inc. in Penniston to create employment for rural farmers hit hard by the banana industry's collapse. We made bamboo ceiling facing and later all kinds of utilitarian items from local materials.

I learned so much from all these ventures that I cannot separate them from the work I do now, which focuses on developing a creative and productive harmonious relationship between wo/man and the landscape. I have single parented two children which has been in no small measure an indispensable training for my work with the youth, particularly in understanding what our youngsters are capable of, if nurtured to realize their special gifts for our communities.

Q. *What work do you do presently?*

VR: My current projects all interrelate and stimulate eachother and in a nutshell are:

Creative teaching - In 2001 I set up the Cambridge A-level Art and Design programme at St. Vincent and the Grenadines

Community College and despite constraints regarding space, equipment and materials, it is designed specifically to stimulate the creative consciousness of the youth starting with the cultural context of their Vincentian experience. We work with creative project development, starting with observational drawing and continuing towards a resolution, drawing on oral, visual and written research. The course is constantly evolving; it encompasses ecology and guides students through their creative development with a comprehension of nature as a source of ideas and inspiration, as well as growing a connection with their communal historical heritage. An outcome is, of course, a maturation of the student into an environmentally conscious being capable of organized creative action.

In 2004 the art students formed a group called CYAM Contemporary Young Artists' Movement embarking on socially responsible projects (art exhibitions/ gallery/ art activities for children/mural painting/ tree planting/ working with SVG National Trust.)

The group also raised funds for art materials and their example has spurred many other youngsters into action- we try to build cooperation and understanding as well as get excellent exam results which enables students to take the next step in further studies.

As an outcome of the A-level programme, we have a growing creative community, of youngsters studying overseas (efforts to source scholarships for them is ongoing), pursuing further studies in environmental design, theatre, film, art education, fashion design, media studies, graphic design and fine arts. Many are doing amazing work locally teaching in every highschool that offers Visual arts at CXC level. So they are making a contribution locally on the development of creative education- I can vouch for their considerable input as I inherit many of their students on the A level course!

Also in the field of education, In 2008 I was invited to lecture on the BFA programme at the University of the West Indies' Errol Barrow Centre of the Creative Imagination in Barbados in the area of creative project development and have designed a creativity course for the same centre.

In June 2007 the college students and I launched a weekly radio programme called The Art Room- the first radio programme hosted by the youth in St. Vincent. Its focus is on the role of creativity in society, raising awareness among the youth and has dealt with various topics pertinent to the strengthening of community relations through collective, creative problem solving. It has helped the students build their confidence through participatory discussion, and to impress the general public with the ideas of the youth. Since June 2009 the programme has been hosted by NBC radio station.

In the field of creative education, I also conducted in-service training for 80 primary and secondary school teachers and 21 student teachers in creative teaching methodologies for the EU/Ministry of Education and assisted the Ministry of Education on the development of the National Curriculum Creative Arts as well as writing a teacher's guide for implementation of the curriculum. In 2008, I was delighted to assist the Ministry of Culture set up the first visual arts exhibition for SVG at Carifesta- comprising 34 pieces, from 17 artists of all backgrounds and ages.

Another activity I am involved in is farmer/gardening. I began growing vegetables when I arrived in St. Vincent and became a certified farmer in 1997. I farmed bananas on two acres for several years, mainly with a view to cultivating the fibre for paper making and handcraft. I had an aversion to using any chemicals, as was then the common practice, and researched into how the previous generations used to feed entire families off the 'yam piece'. That held the clue to the type of farming I wanted to do and I learned a lot from elders in my community about this traditional farming knowledge. At an earth building/land regeneration workshop in Mexico in 2003, I was introduced to permaculture by Albert Bates, of The Farm Ecovillage, and what appealed to me about it was that it brought my design background and farming together. I had studied pattern language through cell histology during my MA course in the UK and subsequently conducted research into traditional aesthetics in Japan. I discovered that the relationships of interdependency explored in my artwork, were echoed in this integrated approach to regenerating the earth. I now practice natural farming as a creative process starting with direct observation and building productive systems through soil enrichment-which ultimately means doing what will nurture the earthworm population! It's amazing how simple and yet how productive this system can be, as productive as artificial farming methods, but it's sustainable- healing the soil instead of destroying it.

My passion and reverence for nature underlies all the work I do and finds flow and expression through my natural garden and earth building. I pursue these projects mostly single-handedly. They are my creative works like painting, drawing and sculpture, using the plants and earth as the medium. These are special places for me, where there is only harmony and observation of the intelligence of nature. Many insights are revealed there. One guiding principle is that we have to put in to take out. Our taking from nature without this consciousness of putting in is the root of all of our problems- that are based in lack of compassion.

I think of myself as an "intuitive" gardener. The natural garden has its own fascinating story where everything plays a part, and I work with what is there, or rather it works through me. It holds an evolving story through attention to it and though different in approach to our Hand2Earth educational project, much of what I learn in the intuitive garden is offered to Hand2Earth.

The essence of what I do in that space is, I suppose, is to see how we can create, with nature as our guide, the healing energy of the mountaintop. And it's a space I have always been pulled towards so strongly, that to remain in communication with humans is actually a real effort at times!! But of course that is necessary and important work for we are all part of each other in this wonderful beautiful life of ours.

However, I do envisage a time when I shall indeed retreat into nature and remain there to learn many more of her secrets, I only feel like I have skimmed the surface!

Q: What are your recommendations for empowering the youth?

VR: To do this successfully and productively we must first understand them- it's a fact that most youngsters have an acute sense of displacement due to compromised socialization. They are ambitious and yet confused. They are all driven to accomplish, some more obviously than others.

So what I try to do is help them through creative endeavour to find a feeling of connection, a sense of belonging that can only come through a process of self-realization and to help them see that this sense is intrinsically linked with their environment. Once you have this connection upon which you can build a love of beauty in their surroundings and nature (that is inherent, so we are only awakening it), then they can become excited about working with the arts and their environment, take an interest in their heritage and what has been done before, and realize that they can contribute to creating change through designing and using technology sustainably. The belief that they can make a difference feeds their drive and gives them direction. Obviously this cannot be done with words alone, but through action. The challenge is how to structure that path to empowerment for them.

One of the major stumbling blocks I have found to working with the youth and other groups in St Vincent and the Grenadines, is that people don't trust each other; this lack of trust is based on their own experience, which is of course valid. As a result individual differences, dishonesty, and insecurities undermine group undertakings. The process of self-realization is critical to build trust from within so that the individual becomes able to safely view multiple perspectives without feeling threatened. This can be established through creative teaching, constant reassurance and use of analogies while working with youngsters. The experience of working in a group is critical in realizing the trust necessary to proceed.

I have found that some of the youngsters and adults I have worked with, are so full of self-doubt that they don't believe the positive reinforcement I give them. Eventually, when they realize I do truly believe in them (this can take months in some cases) and what they can accomplish, they become visibly more determined and confident. As we build groups that have come through the process together, they are more trustful, form life-long friendships (this is important to work together in the future from that same bond of trust) and can then be an example to other youths.

The third principle after understanding how they feel and building trust is appreciating that children learn from each other. Youngsters learn best from self-organization- they need to feel that they are making discoveries and doing something new, which is why the way we have presented many subjects to them, including farming, doesn't appeal.

I try to establish an interactive forum and learning environment where they can discover through their own actions and transmit these discoveries to others. This is why the Hand2Earth project is essentially youth driven- the project is to be a way for them to find out and reflect, act, create and produce.

Of course, in the context of the many global challenges that this young generation will face, we cannot be said to be educating young people unless we teach them how to work together. They are already well-trained in networking and if we can harness these skills to a sense of social responsibility, they will be better equipped to deal with the economic and environmental crises that are the pressing global challenges poised to impact hard on small developing island nations.

The cycle of life is strongly perceptible when working with the youth and things are 'flowing', one feels a sense of continuity. For example- one of my students, Rose-Marie Lewis, who graduated from college in 2005, was in the children's classes I set up years ago- she was 6 years old then. After graduation she taught for two years in secondary schools, where she got great results with her CXC art students and she is currently studying for a Bachelor of Arts degree in Jamaica. Just one person's story. It's also been an amazing experience for me to see present students, Olivia Stephens and Chante Ferdinand, start to teach weekly art classes for children. They were just one or two years old when I started working with children. In a flash, the years have gone by. And now I feel like the child!!

Q: How would you summarize all this in terms of what you have achieved?

VR: There is great satisfaction to being able to step back and see something not only continue but continue to grow- I feel that is what I am working towards with the intuitive garden and the youth.

I guess the measurement of success is in direct proportion to the distance I can step away and feel the growth gradually increasing. There will be a time, when I can retreat to my spiritual home forever, of no further consequence and that will be the measurement of ultimate success. So my ramblings have taken me back to the beginning where I may well have answered my own doubts over whether I have successfully moved forward!

References

1. Ivan Illich, Vernacular Values, *CoEvolution Quarterly*, 1980. The essays were the basis of Illich's book, *Shadow Work* (Marion Boyars, 1981)
2. Paul Klee, Ways of Studying Nature, *Paul Klee's Notebooks, Volume 1- Essays*, 1923.
3. Earl Lovelace, Culture and the Environment, *The New Aesthetic and the Meaning of Culture in the Caribbean – proceedings of the CARIFESTA V Symposia*, Editor Pearl Eintou Springer, 1995.
4. David Bohm, Donald Factor and Peter Garrett, *Dialogue- A Proposal*, 1991. http://www.ratical.com/many_worlds/K/dialogueProposal.html#7
5. *Searchlight*, Interactive Media Ltd, St. Vincent and the Grenadines.
6. John Stewart, Aesthetics and the Early Baptist Church, *The New Aesthetic and the Meaning of Culture in the Caribbean – proceedings of the CARIFESTA V Symposia*, , Editor Pearl Eintou Springer, 1995.
7. Lloyd Best, Development Issues and the Regional Imagination, *The New Aesthetic and the Meaning of Culture in the Caribbean – proceedings of the*

CARIFESTA V Symposia, Editor Pearl Eintou Springer, 1995
8. Shemon Baptiste, graduating Class 2009, St. Vincent and the Grenadines Community College, Division of Arts, Sciences and General Studies.
9. Excerpt from an article by Christophe Joseph, www.dominica-weekly.com
10. John Pickford, Aging Gracefully in Dominica, *From Our Own Correspondent,* www.bbc.CARIBBEAN.com
11. CARICOM, Caribbean Community, formerly the Caribbean Free Trade Association (CARIFTA) formed in 1972 at the Seventh Heads of Government Conference, providing for the free movement of labour and capital and coordination of agricultural, industrial and foreign policies.
12. Russell |Smith Sc. D, *Tree Crops: A Permanent Agriculture:* Chapter 1, Harcourt, Brace, 1929
13. Proyecto San Isidro Educacion Permanente, Tlaxco, Tlaxcala.
14. John Roulac, *Backyard Composting,* Green Earth Books, 1999.
15. Strategy, Forethought and Insight: An Online Journal, www.sfisvg.com
16. Gordon Browne: *A Clear Agenda for Reform in 2010,* www.huffingtonpost.com
17. Masanobu Fukuoka, *The One-Straw Revolution*, Other India Press, 1992
18. FAO Carib-Agri is a service provided by the FAO Sub-Regional Office, Barbados. www.fao.org
19. Bill Mollison, *Introduction to Permaculture,* 1991.
20. Caribbean Development Bank. 1998. *Report of the Caribbean Regional Workshop on sustainable development indicators,* held at the Grand Barbados Hotel, Barbados, October 22-23, 1998.

21. An event organized by the author, an outcome of which was the production of an anthology of art and poetry by Vincentian women *Seen and Heard,* Hobo Jungle Press, 2011, sponsored by the Embassy of Bolivarian Republic of Venezuela, in St.Vincent and the Grenadines.
22. Alvin Morrow, *Breaking the Curse of Willie Lynch,* Rising Sun Publications, 2003
23. Myles Horton and Paolo Friere, *We Make the Road by Walking- Conversations on Education and Social Change;* Temple University Press 1990
24. As quoted in "What Life Means to Einstein : An Interview by George Sylvester Viereck" in *The Saturday Evening Post,* Vol. 202 (26 October 1929), p. 117
25. Mihali Csikszentmihali, *Creativity, Fulfilment and Flow,* TED talks, 2004, www.TED.com
26. Marie-Louise Von Franz, *Projection & Recollection in Jungian psychology: 106*
27. Masanobu Fukuoka, *The Road Back to Nature, Regaining the Paradise Lost,* Japan Publications Inc., 1987
28. Miles Horton and Paolo Friere, *We Make the Road By Walking- Conversations on Education and Social Change;* Temple University Press 1990, Chapter 4.
29. Edward Kamau Brathwaite, *The Dream Coming in with the Rain, The New Aesthetic and the Meaning of Culture in the Caribbean – proceedings of the CARIFESTA V Symposia,* Editor Pearl Eintou Springer, 1995.
30. "The Art Room", weekly interactive radio programme on Saturday afternoons, National Broadcasting Corporation, www.nbcsvg.com
31. www.officialkwanzaawebsite.org
32. The Garifuna name for St. Vincent, meaning, "the beauty of the rainbows in the Valleys."

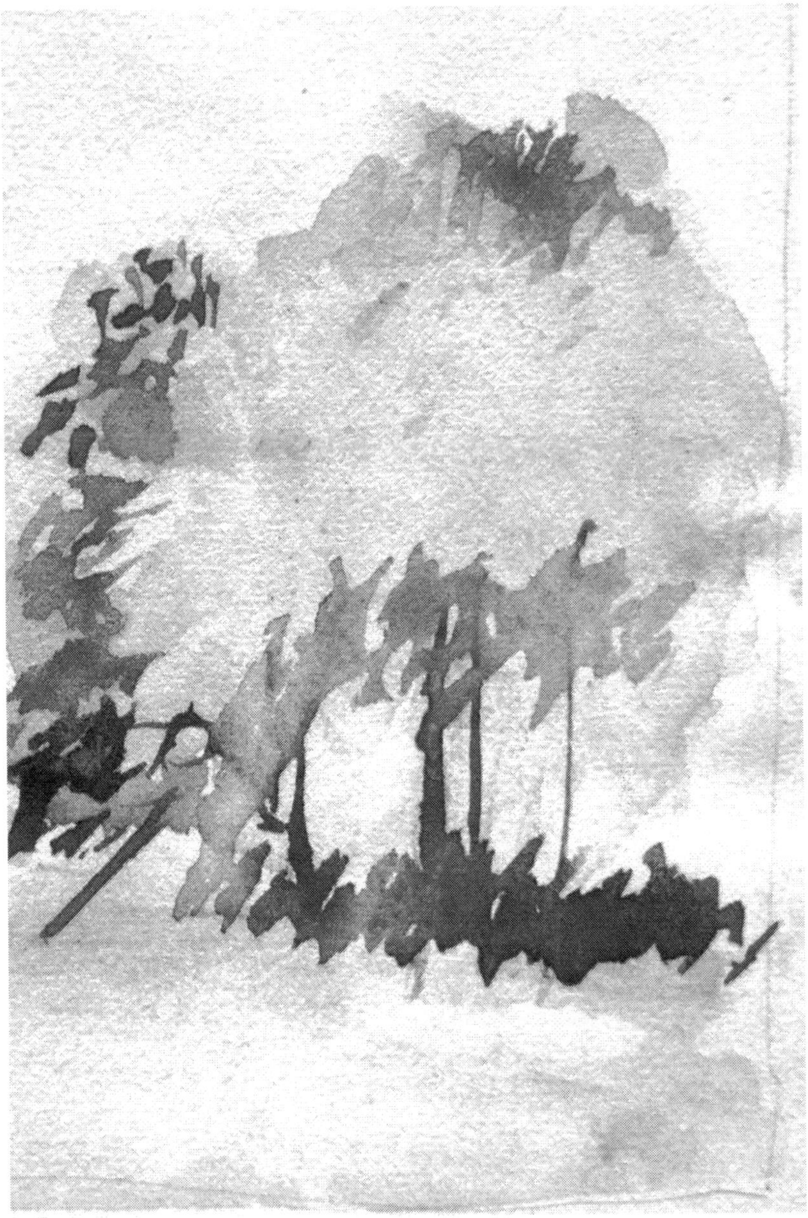

About The Author

Vonnie Roudette, MA, is a visual artist with over twenty-five years experience as a creative educator facilitating courses for children, degree students, handcraft producers and teachers. Educated in Manchester, UK, she subsequently researched traditional aesthetics at Kyoto Arts University, Japan and joined Issey Miyake's design team in Tokyo before freelancing as a textile and theatre designer in Europe. She has exhibited her paintings, drawings, prints and textiles in Osaka, Tokyo, London and the Caribbean.

After several years balancing free-lance design work with part-time lecturing in the Faculty of Art at Manchester Metropolitan University and Berkshire College of Art and Design, Roudette relocated to her father's birthplace, Trinidad and Tobago, with her two young children in 1992 and later that year arrived in the Caribbean islands of St. Vincent and the Grenadines (SVG).

Motivated by the absence of creative education in the islands' schools, she began facilitating creative educational programs for children. Between 1996-2001, as handcraft development consultant to the OAS Heritage Tourism Project, she provided training in design development and marketing to craft producers in SVG, St. Lucia, St. Kitts and Nevis. In 1996 she co-founded SVG CREATE, an NGO for Vincentian artists and craft producers. A year later, she established Fibreworks Inc, a craft factory in Penniston, rural St. Vincent that provided skills and employment to over thirty-five producers from neighbouring village communities.

Roudette has collaborated with various Departments of Government in SVG since 1994 to provide locally based solutions for economic, cultural, social and environmental challenges facing small-island developing states. She designed the National Handcraft Development Plan (2001), the visual arts component of the national curriculum, facilitated the introduction of creative teaching methods through teacher training (2007), and was SVG's first visual arts coordinator to CARIFESTA X (2008).

A practicing natural builder and certified farmer in St. Vincent, Roudette pioneered the introduction of tertiary art and design education to the island's Community College in 2001, which recently expanded to the Associate's Degree course in Fine Arts, Design and Cultural Communications. The course links art with the environment, offering creative education for sustainable development and fosters community relations to reinstate cultural heritage through the transfer of intergenerational skills and knowledge.

Roudette has organized more than twenty national exhibitions of creative arts and handcrafts in St. Vincent, of which 'Seen and Heard' (June 2009) spawned the first publication of Vincentian women artists' painting and poetry. (Hobo Jungle Press, 2011.)

Active since 1994 as a social commentator in weekly newspapers and on national radio, her growing following of readers and listeners requested copies of the commentaries; this first collection of essays is Roudette's response.

She currently resides on her natural farm in Penniston, St. Vincent, teaches at SVG Community College and coordinates Hand2Earth, a rural educational sustainability lifestyles project.

www.naturalbelonger.wordpress.com

Printed in Great Britain
by Amazon.co.uk, Ltd.,
Marston Gate.